I0623669

MONETI$ED

*Mastering the Modern Dating Market,
Building Legacy, and Leveraging Life
for maximum Power and Purpose.*

Anthony R Barber Jr

Dedicated to

My Sons
"Sebastian & Amari"
I got now...you got next...

CONTENTS

INTRODUCTION

Greetings to all, that unbiasedly choose to read my offering to the modern relationship landscape. I trust many that reading this will find some clarity within the pages, and I'm more than sure you'll gain a new perspective to add to your frame of reference. First off, I spent the better part of twelve years in a marriage I thought for the most part was solid, and it only took six months for me to realize how fragile my perceptions of relationship dynamics between males and females were. Before you say the typical easy-button statements such as, "who hurt you?", The answer to that question is simple..." I did". I'm completely at fault for how my marriage turned out at the end of the day. I didn't honor, or value my time, energy, attention, and money that way I needed to. I poured untold amounts of affection, guidance, protection, and provision to a secret enemy the whole time. Funny part is I seen it from the beginning, and ignored all red flags presented, even though they were sporadic in nature and event based. The fact I went against my gut feelings, my intuition, and basic logic is my "L" to hold as it caused me to do some deep self-maintenance and re-evaluation of priorities. I'm an Ambitious workaholic that linked up and gave my last name to a woman with zero ability to nurture my spirt, assist me in any practical way when comes to business and or investment, and who wielded her own personal trauma as a weapon over the years. I let a "crash-out" succubus latch on to me and she fed off my energy for over a decade and did nothing but complain about life as I helped her improve while being depleted simultaneously. During my time in the relationship I started several small side businesses, amasses a 7-figure net worth via investment vehicles, and wrote four books. We also have two children(son's) together also, so that makes things very interesting moving forward to say the least. Trust me, I did my best to vet my ex-wife as thoroughly as possible, which is why our first child wasn't born until five years into the relationship. I obviously had doubts about the validity of my then girlfriends' intentions, but me being born with a brain that likes to sink its teeth into challenges, I ignored obvious red flags. Ultimately, I'm at fault for engaging with a broken human and trying to play the role "Mr. fix it", even though my discipline is aerospace and finance. I had no business trying to repair another person with unaddressed psychological issues. What did I get for my troubles, you may ask, and I'm happy to say I gained knowledge, insight, perspective, wisdom, and of course hindsight along that journey. Don't get me wrong, it wasn't a complete loss in my view, considering she wasn't able to take me out like her and my mother had planned. I'll expound on this further in the book as we go on. I learned just how important fathers are in their children's lives growing up, as my ex-wife had a very distant relationship with her father to say the least. She was neglected by the first man that was tasked to protect, guide, and provide for her wellbeing. The man (her father) not only dropped the ball, but he chooses to stab the emotional ballon to eliminate any air of affection that perhaps was available. Looking back (via hindsight) I was psychotic for diving into that ring of psychoanalysis to punch above my weight in the name of love.

Towards the end of the journey, I could clearly see I wasn't going to be able to pull the nose up on this thing, and a crash was imminent, yet still, I learned things over the twelve years prior to her crashing out and during the battle that followed. I learned for all the typical trip wires and traps I allowed myself to fall into. I remember something I told my cousin prior to my ex-wife and I moving in with one another..." I must do this to evolve. "My willingness to stare into the jaws of death and fight off it's cold embrace is what ultimately led to me writing this book based on my prior dating habits, my twelve years of marriage, my new role as a father, and my re-entrance back into this new Monetized dating marketplace.

At the time of me writing this book, the Gender wars have officially begun in the western hemisphere. This battle has been raging for roughly twelve years since around 2012, at the dawn of the "online dating market." Fast forward to today, and we are now fully stepping into "the monetized dating market" as I write this book. Many individuals miss the direct correlation between these trends and the societal shifts that took place during the global pandemic that kicked off in 2020. Forced to sit still for over a year, many people had the opportunity to reflect on their lives and consider the direction they truly wanted to take. Others experienced a rude awakening as they confronted their unhappiness—not only within their careers or financial situations but also in their relationships. In this new landscape, the rules of engagement have changed. The monetized dating market challenges men to rethink their approach to relationships, requiring a combination of self-discipline, emotional intelligence, and value-building. No longer can individuals rely solely on charm or physical appearance; success now demands a deeper understanding of oneself and the dynamics of play in modern dating. Self-discipline is essential in navigating the complexities of this marketplace, allowing men to focus on personal growth, build resilience, and establish clear goals. Emotional intelligence is equally vital, as understanding one's emotions and those of potential partners can lead to more meaningful connections. Lastly, value-building—whether through financial stability, career advancement, or personal development—empowers men to present themselves not only as attractive partners in a highly competitive environment but as stoic men of purpose. MONETI$ED will guide you through these critical themes, equipping you with the tools to leverage your life for maximum gain in both personal and romantic endeavors. Together, we will explore the intricate interplay of self-management, financial acumen, and the psychology of Modern dating, enabling you to thrive in this rapidly evolving landscape. You must understand, overstand, and inner stand what is taking place around you in real time Gentlemen. The adaptation or die concept is deeply interwoven into this modern era.

01

MONETIZED DATING

Historical Era Vs. Modern Era

Often, we find ourselves looking for comfort and clarity whenever events happen that effectively turn our previous mindset on its ear in an instant. That's what happened to me once I realized the modern dating market is no new thing, but a remixed version of historical female human nature. Theres nothing new under the sun as king Solomon so wisely put it, and in terms of the dating landscape goes, that statement reigns supreme. Once I took a deep dive into historical accounts of the landscape the truth began revealing itself to me slowly but surely. From ancient times (**Ancient Civilizations**), relationships between men and women have often been transactional in nature. For example, in many early societies, marriages were arranged for political alliances, economic stability, and social status. Women, while often lacking direct access to resources, utilized their roles as wives or mothers to influence their families' fortunes. This speaks directly to a woman subtle yet effective nature as it relates to manipulating men. For instance, in ancient Mesopotamia, women were sometimes expected to marry for economic gain, with dowries serving as a form of leverage. Women could wield significant power behind the scenes, ensuring their families prospered through strategic marital alliances. During the Middle Ages (**The Medieval Period**), the practice of courtly love emerged, where romantic pursuits often intertwined with social status and financial security. Women of noble birth used their attractiveness and social skills to gain advantages, securing favorable marriages that provided access to wealth and land. The concept of chivalry elevated the role of women as objects of desire, incentivizing men to compete for their attention and resources. The **(Renaissance and Enlightenment Period)** marked a shift towards individualism and romantic love, but economic considerations still played a crucial role in relationships. Women used their desirability and social connections to secure advantageous marriages. With the rise of the bourgeois class during the Enlightenment, the marriage market became more competitive. Women sought to position themselves strategically, leveraging their beauty and intellect to attract wealthy suitors, thereby solidifying their social standing and financial security. Then came **(The Industrial Revolution)** As societies transitioned from agrarian to industrial economies in the 18th and 19th centuries, dating began to take on a more modern form. The emergence of the middle class created new opportunities for women to seek upward mobility through marriage. Courtship rituals became more formalized, and women learned to navigate social expectations to attract men with resources. The advent of dating as a social activity also led to the rise of romantic love, where women used their allure to draw men into relationships that offered both emotional and financial benefits.

The early **(20th century)** saw significant social changes, including women's suffrage movement and increased workforce participation. Despite these advancements, traditional dating norms persisted, often placing the onus on women to attract and maintain relationships with financially stable men. The **"marriage market"** concept gained traction, with women being advised to marry up economically as many are seeking to don now in modern times. Fast forward past the post-World War II boom, dating has become more commercialized, with matchmaking services such as (Christian Mingle) and later online dating platforms such as (Tinder) emerging, allowing women to strategically leverage their dating choices for resource acquisition. With these new social platforms emerging came the Rise of Online Dating and the Monetized Dating Market. In the late 20th and early 21st centuries, the

ANTHONY R BARBER JR.

internet revolutionized dating dynamics. Online dating platforms commodified relationships, creating a marketplace where individuals could market themselves to potential partners. Women began to wield their social capital more effectively, leveraging profiles and photos to attract men who could provide financial stability or emotional support. As dating apps gained popularity, the monetized dating market emerged, with women often adopting strategies to extract resources through selective dating practices, including the "alpha male" phenomenon, and "high value man" tier where women pursued high-status men with the most significant resources. Expanding the theme with modern examples of powerful men being manipulated or influenced by toxic or manipulative women offers a clear view of how these dynamics continue to shape relationships today. While the seduction and subtle charm may have evolved with technology and media, the essence of manipulation and resource extraction remains. In the current dating landscape, where relationships are being monetized left and right, you've got to understand the toll it's taking on a man's time, energy, attention, and—ultimately—his wallet. And the crazy part?

Clinical and psychological research is showing exactly how this market drains men dry, taking from them what could be channeled into real self-growth and advancement, in exchange from playing a deadly chess game with the opposite sex.

1. The Swipe Game is Hijacking Your Mind

Apps like Tinder and Hinge are playing with your dopamine system, locking you into cycles of swipes and matches that do nothing for your future. They're designed to keep you hooked on that instant gratification, feeding your brain small hits of dopamine every time you match. According to The Journal of Social and Clinical Psychology, this leads to a reliance on short-term rewards, weakening your discipline and undermining your long-term happiness. It's no wonder so many men get caught up, wasting hours that should be fueling their grind on these fleeting interactions instead.

2. The Toll of Superficial Interactions

Most of what you get in this market isn't meaningful, it's transactional. And this wears on you. Studies from Cyberpsychology, Behavior, and Social Networking reveal how these apps push users into a "choice overload." More options don't mean better results; they lead to paralysis, indecision, and ultimately, dissatisfaction. Men invest their emotional energy in something that barely scratches the surface, leaving them drained and disillusioned. Instead of feeling fulfilled, they're worn out from constantly chasing these shallow connections.

3. Your Finances, Caught in the Game

Let's talk about the money trap. Between paying for app upgrades to stand out and the never-ending pressure to impress on dates, men are bleeding cash in this game. The Journal of Economic Behavior & Organization makes it clear: spending on fleeting interactions doesn't come close to the ROI you'd get from investing in yourself or a business venture. While you're out there covering premium subscriptions and fancy dinners, that cash could build your empire. This market is a high-cost, low-reward arena, and too many men are caught in the loop without realizing the real price they're paying.

4. The Cycle of Idealization and Burnout

Constant app use feeds unrealistic expectations. According to Psychological Bulletin, heavy users start expecting perfection with each swipe, always thinking the next match will be "the one." This constant search builds frustration and disappointment because reality never meets these sky-high expectations. Many end up on a hamster wheel, emotionally burnt out from trying to find meaning in a system that isn't built for anything deeper than surface-level interaction. It's psychological damage that adds up overtime, leaving you feeling more alone and less motivated. We must detox from the technology of the times, especially if you're not utilizing it to better yourself in some way.

5. Transactional Culture = Emotional Detachment

The monetized dating culture trains men to view relationships through a transactional lens, which leads to emotional detachment. This isn't just theory—studies from the Journal of Interpersonal Relations have proven that when relationships become transactional, true intimacy fades. Over time, men experience what's known as "dating fatigue"—an exhaustion from constantly feeling like you're on the clock, paying out with no real return. For men who are about their purpose and self-growth, this detachment is draining. You end up emotionally spent, unable to connect in any real way, and left wondering why the fulfillment you're looking for feels further out of reach. In the end, the monetized dating market may promise abundance, but it's delivering scarcity when it comes to real rewards. The data backs it up: the toll on a man's mental health, wallet, and energy isn't worth what little this market has to offer. For men who are serious about grinding and building something meaningful, shifting focus away from this system and back onto self-investment and growth leads to a richer, more fulfilling life—on your own terms. This is how you build; this is how you stop letting a system designed to drain you win.

The SUM

In the modern era, just as in ancient times, powerful men have been brought down by their inability to control their desires and their vulnerability to manipulative or toxic relationships. From political leaders to billionaires and actors, the stories of these men serve as a reminder that obsession and infatuation can blind even the most successful individuals, leading to personal and professional ruin. The unlimited options available now provided females an avenue for a more expansive relationship lifestyle. They no longer were pigeon-held to only dealing with the male prospects within a certain geographical zone. This technology effectively helped woman gain not only a clear foothold on the marketplace, but it also allowed for never-before-seen levels of transparency in the market as it stands today.

Women want a man over 6ft can now shop around not just the country where they reside but essentially the whole global marketplace was opened to them in general, especially when they started to leverage popular platforms like "Instagram". Amid motivational video rants, sports highlight reels, and movie scene snippets lies a hypersexual digital redlight district of sorts. Once you feed the algorithm with your likes and preferences, you'll be served large portions of fleshly delights. That same pseudo–Digital Redlight district has transformed into a literal redlight district with platforms like "Only fans", not to mention the girls that make it very clear they are for sale via links, emails, and phone numbers on full display for any potential clients that come along. Throughout history, women have leveraged their positions in various ways to influence men and extract resources. From strategic marriages to the modern monetized dating market, the interplay of social media dynamics, economic considerations, and personal agency has shaped relationships and dating practices. Today, as the landscape evolves, understanding these historical contexts can illuminate current trends and empower men and women to navigate relationships with greater awareness and strategy. As a man, you must get very clear on which rung of the dating hierarchy ladder your currently gripping.

02 |

THE DUALITY OF NATURE
Force vs. Subtlety

Relationships, at their core, aren't achievements, milestones, or status symbols. Strip away the glossy surface, and their fundamentally primal blend of instincts, desires, and subconscious drives. For all the religious ideals, cultural scripts, and social expectations that surround relationships, they're still grounded in nature's basic wiring. Yet many men wake up each day trying to turn a relationship into some sort of status trophy, pushing to "win" a woman as though she were an accolade. This approach might have made sense in times when people had limited exposure to the outside world—when travel was difficult, communities were isolated, and relationships were chosen from a small pool within a single town or village. But in today's world, that's a fantasy, one that technology has all but shattered. Today, with a smartphone in your pocket, the whole world is accessible in seconds. The endless scroll of social media offers a curated highlight reel of life, love, and attraction, making everything in our immediate environment seem somehow lesser in comparison. Why focus on your partner's flaws, quirks, and imperfections when there's an infinite parade of picture-perfect faces, bodies, and personas just a tap away? Feeling uninspired by your partner? You can log into your favorite app, lose yourself in an endless loop of visual appeal, and "escape" reality without ever leaving your couch. Want a more immersive experience? Pay a small fee and access even more curated content, drawing you deeper into a world that's tailored for temporary satisfaction. We've all become participants in our collective discontent. By indulging these virtual fantasies, we feed an insatiable appetite for novelty and thrill, while our real-world connections become stale and unsatisfying by comparison. In an age when stimulation is readily available, we're blurring the lines between need and want, between real connection and hollow attention. In this digital ecosystem, relationships are no longer driven by necessity but by choice, and often a volatile, fleeting choice at that. The endless supply of options has created a paradox where nothing ever seems to measure up. Men who try to "force" a relationship, who chase the traditional ideal of a relationship as a badge of honor, are ignoring the subtle truth of today's environment: relationships are about balancing authenticity with adaptability. Force in relationships creates tension, subtlety breeds adaptability. Those who can maneuver these new dynamics with ease and finesse will thrive, while those who are stuck in outdated models will find themselves endlessly dissatisfied.

Research even points to the impact of this endless choice and instant gratification on relationship satisfaction. A study in the Journal of Personality and Social Psychology noted that too many options can lead to decision fatigue, regret, and dissatisfaction. With the rise of dating apps and social media, the "paradox of choice" means that often, people are left wondering if there's someone better out there, even if they're with a good partner. And this fuels a cycle where relationships become disposable, "just for now" options rather than lasting commitments. Theres a Subtle Art when it comes to Building Real Value in the marketplace. The only way to counter this new cycle is by taking a step back from the superficial and recognizing the value of genuine connections, something that, ironically, has become rare in this hyperconnected era. True confidence and self-worth are rooted in understanding your own strengths and values, not in how many "likes" you can collect or who's on your arm for show. Men who understand this don't need to "force" their relationships to fit a mold, nor do they feel pressured to constantly consume and compare. They know that fulfillment isn't found through shallow indulgence or a forced connection. It's about subtlety, patience, and recognizing what aligns with your life purpose. In essence, our digital age has forced men to adapt or remain lost in the illusion. A man who moves with subtlety and purpose values what he builds, without needing it to be flaunted or put on display. Relationships, in this way, are less about claiming a status symbol and more about finding someone who complements the journey. And that's a truth that stands out, even when the world seems fixated on the opposite.

Directness and Conquest

Historically, men have been shaped by evolutionary pressures to adopt a direct and forceful approach to relationships. In ancient times, survival and reproduction required men to be aggressive hunters, warriors, and protectors. This is translated into a straightforward, action-oriented way of engaging with the world. Men sought to conquer both in battle and in courtship, often viewing romantic pursuits through the lens of competition and dominance. In many cultures, men proved their worth through displays of power, wealth, or physical prowess—traits that signaled their ability to provide and protect. This direct nature led men to view relationships as achievements, often failing to recognize the subtle strategies employed by women to influence outcomes. Men, driven by their competitive instincts and biological drives, were frequently susceptible to visual cues such as beauty, charm, and sensuality. This one-dimensional focus on winning a woman's favor or sexual access left them vulnerable to manipulation through more indirect tactics.

Subtlety and Influence

On the other hand, women have historically operated within different constraints. Lacking direct access to power in many societies, women developed more subtle and indirect methods to secure resources and influence outcomes. From an evolutionary standpoint, women's reproductive role demanded that they prioritize security, stability, and resource acquisition. Since physical aggression was often unavailable as a tool for women, they learned to use their intellect, charm, and sexuality to shape their environments in less overt ways. In relationships, women have often relied on seduction, emotional intelligence, and psychological manipulation to attract and keep men of status and resources. Their strategies are rooted in appealing to men's desires and instincts—particularly their need for validation, admiration, and sexual gratification. Throughout history, powerful men have been brought to their knees by women who used their beauty and cunning to subtly extract influence, wealth, and social standing, often without the men realizing they were being leveraged. Women's ability to charm and seduce men has been one of the most powerful tools in the subtle art of relationship negotiation. The feminine archetype of the "femme fatale" dates to ancient myths and stories of powerful women who could bend the wills of men through charm and beauty. From Cleopatra's legendary influence over Julius Caesar and Mark Antony, to the courtesans of Renaissance Europe, history is filled with examples of men in power being led into compromising situations by women who appeared to be delicate and harmless. The key to this manipulation lies in women's mastery of emotional intelligence and intuition. Women have a natural ability to read body language, gauge a man's emotional state, and tailor their behavior to disarm his defenses. A woman might feign vulnerability or innocence to gain a man's trust, leading him to feel protective or desired, which in turn compels him to provide for her emotionally or materially. Men, in their haste to secure affection or intimacy, often overlook the calculated nature of these interactions, confusing a woman's charm with genuine affection.

The Power of Illusion

Men, driven by a desire to impress, are often blinded by their need to conquer and attain a woman's favor. This creates a dynamic where they are more focused on the immediate goal of winning the woman's approval and admiration rather than analyzing the broader context of the relationship. A

13

woman's indirect methods—flattery, seduction, emotional vulnerability—act as a smokescreen, leading men to believe they are in control when they are being skillfully guided. Historically, women have leveraged this dynamic to extract resources without appearing overtly demanding. By maintaining an air of mystery or playing hard to get, women create a sense of scarcity, encouraging men to compete and invest more resources in the pursuit. Whether through the allure of beauty, intelligence, or the promise of intimacy, women have often led men to overestimate the emotional connection, while subtly redirecting the focus toward securing their own needs—whether it's financial security, social status, or protection.

Men's failure to recognize these subtle manipulations has led to countless instances of misallocated resources, unbalanced relationships, High divorce rate and even loss of power, and leverage Throughout history, men have been distracted from their primary goals, sidelined from decision-making, or drained of wealth due to the seductive influence of women operating through indirect channels. Whether kings who lost kingdoms or wealthy men who squandered fortunes, history is filled with examples of men overextending themselves, only to realize too late the true cost of their blind pursuit. Fast-forward to today's dating market, and the same dynamics continue to play out, albeit in a more sophisticated form. In the age of social media, dating apps, and digital courtship, women still wield the power of charm, seduction, and emotional subtlety to attract and retain so-called high-value men especially when you add it modern-day plastic surgery procedures, and technology that filters the true form of an individual. The rise of "hypergamy" (the practice of women marrying or dating up) is a direct result of women using these ancient tactics in a modern context, leading men to invest heavily in relationships that may ultimately benefit the woman more than themselves. This subtle warfare between men's direct nature and women's indirect methods has always existed, but in today's monetized dating market, the stakes are higher than ever. Understanding these dynamics is key for men looking to navigate this complex arena without falling prey to manipulation.

Let us briefly touch on a few historical accounts of powerful men who were manipulated and ultimately knocked out of position due to their obsession with toxic or manipulative women. These examples highlight the consequences of falling prey to seduction, charm, and subtle manipulation, often leading to the downfall of once-great men:

Julius Caesar and Cleopatra (44 BCE)

One of the most famous historical examples is Julius Caesar's relationship with Cleopatra, the last active ruler of the Ptolemaic Kingdom of Egypt. Cleopatra was known for her beauty, intelligence, and political acumen, and she used these traits to entangle Caesar in a passionate affair that ultimately served her interests. Cleopatra needed Roman support to maintain her throne, and through her relationship with Caesar, she secured not only his favor but also Roman military protection. Caesar, captivated by Cleopatra's charm and seduction, became deeply involved in her political affairs. He fathered a son with Cleopatra and, in his obsession, allowed her influence to cloud his judgment. His prolonged stay in Egypt and close involvement with Cleopatra aroused suspicion and resentment back in Rome, where many feared, he would attempt to rule as a king with Cleopatra by his side. Caesar's obsession with Cleopatra was one of the factors that contributed to his political downfall. His enemies in the Roman Senate exploited the discontent around his Egyptian escapades, ultimately leading to his assassination in 44 BCE. Cleopatra's subtle manipulation and strategic use of her relationship with Caesar played a key role in destabilizing his position in Rome.

Mark Antony and Cleopatra (31 BCE)

Cleopatra's influence didn't end with Caesar; after his assassination, she set sights on another (Ancient Simp) Mark Antony, one of Rome's most powerful generals and politicians. Like Caesar, Antony became infatuated with Cleopatra and her magnetic allure. Their passionate affair led to Antony neglecting his duties in Rome and prioritizing his life with Cleopatra in Egypt. Cleopatra's manipulations extended beyond personal affairs—she convinced Antony to abandon his political alliances in Rome, leading to a direct conflict with Octavian (the future Augustus Caesar), who viewed Antony's obsession with Cleopatra as a threat to Roman unity. Antony's decision to align himself with Cleopatra, both politically and romantically, resulted in a war with Octavian, culminating in the famous Battle of Actium in 31 BCE. Antony, overconfident and blinded by his attachment to Cleopatra, suffered a crushing defeat. The loss of the battle effectively ended his political career and marked the fall of one of Rome's most influential leaders. Antony's infatuation with Cleopatra ultimately cost him his life and his empire, as he committed suicide after falsely believing that Cleopatra had died. Cleopatra, ever the strategist, attempted to seduce Octavian but, when her advances were rejected, she took her own life. Cleopatra's manipulative charm had led to the downfall of two of the most powerful men in Roman history.

Samson and Delilah (Biblical Account)

One of the most well-known stories of a powerful man being undone by a manipulative woman comes from the biblical tale of Samson and Delilah. Samson, a Nazarite warrior endowed with superhuman strength, was chosen by God to deliver the Israelites from the oppression of the Philistines. His strength, however, was tied to his uncut hair, a secret known only to him. Delilah, a Philistine woman, was sent by the Philistine rulers to discover the source of Samson's strength. Through seduction and manipulation, Delilah gradually wore Samson down, exploiting his affection and desire for her. She repeatedly questioned him about his strength until, in a moment of weakness and obsession, Samson revealed his secret. Delilah immediately betrayed him, cutting his hair while he slept, thus rendering him powerless. Samson's downfall was the result of his obsession with Delilah, who used her charm to manipulate him into revealing his vulnerability. Her betrayal led to his capture, humiliation, and eventual death at the hands of the Philistines. The story of Samson and Delilah serves as a cautionary tale about the dangers of allowing romantic obsession to cloud one's judgment, especially when dealing with a manipulative partner.

King Henry VIII and Anne Boleyn (16th Century)

King Henry VIII's obsession with Anne Boleyn, one of the most famous queens in English history, led to one of the most significant religious and political upheavals of the 16th century. Henry, already married to Catherine of Aragon, became infatuated with Anne, a member of his court, who strategically withheld her affection and refused to become his mistress, unlike many others in his court. Anne used her influence to demand nothing less than becoming queen, forcing Henry to make drastic decisions. Unable to obtain a papal annulment from his first marriage, Henry broke from the Catholic Church and established the Church of England, granting himself the power to divorce Catherine and marry Anne. This decision not only led to religious turmoil but also severely weakened Henry's standing in Europe. Anne's manipulation of Henry's obsession eventually led to her downfall as well. After failing to produce a male heir, Henry grew tired of her and, in a dramatic reversal, had her accused of adultery and treason. Anne was executed in 1536, but her role in manipulating Henry into upending the religious and political order of England left an indelible mark on history.

Louis XV and Madame de Pompadour (18th Century)

Madame de Pompadour, born Jeanne Antoinette Poisson, was a French noblewoman and the official chief mistress of King Louis XV of France. Known for her beauty, intelligence, and political savvy, she wielded considerable influence over the king and, by extension, the French court. Pompadour used her position as Louis's mistress not only to elevate her own status but also to manipulate court politics and secure favors for her allies.

She skillfully charmed Louis, who became infatuated with her despite waning physical interest. Even after their romantic relationship cooled, Pompadour retained significant control over Louis's decisions, positioning herself as his closest confidante and advisor. Many of Louis's decisions, including political appointments and foreign policy choices, were heavily influenced by Pompadour. Her control over him contributed to the weakening of the French monarchy, as she directed resources and attention away from critical matters of state to pursue her own agendas. By the end of Louis's reign, France was mired in financial instability and political discontent, setting the stage for the French Revolution. Pompadour's ability to manipulate and maintain her influence over Louis, despite her fading romantic appeal, serves as a striking example of how a powerful man can be undone by a woman's subtle and strategic influence. While the seduction and subtle charm may have evolved with technology and media, the essence of manipulation and resource extraction remains. Here are several contemporary examples where men, blinded by obsession or infatuation, faced major personal and professional downfalls:

Tiger Woods and His Affairs (2009)

Tiger Woods, one of the most successful and recognizable athletes in history, saw his world unravel due to a series of extramarital affairs that came to light in 2009. At the time, Woods had built a pristine public image as a family man, and his dominance in the world of golf had made him an international icon, amassing millions of dollars in endorsements. However, his numerous affairs with women from various walks of life—some of whom used their charm and seductive power to engage with him—led to one of the biggest public scandals in modern sports. The unraveling of his personal life had severe professional and financial consequences. Not only did his marriage fall apart, but Woods also lost millions in sponsorship deals as brands like Gatorade, AT&T, and Accenture distanced themselves from the scandal. His performance on the golf course also plummeted as he dealt with injuries, a tarnished reputation, and the emotional fallout from the collapse of his personal life. While the women involved may not have directly "manipulated" him in a traditional sense, Woods allowed his desire and obsession to cloud his judgment, ultimately leading to a massive loss of wealth, status, and focus. His story serves as a modern cautionary tale of how powerful men can still be brought down by their unchecked appetites and poor relationship choices.

Bill Clinton and Monica Lewinsky (1998)

One of the most infamous political scandals of the late 20th century was the affair between then-President Bill Clinton and White House intern Monica Lewinsky. Clinton, one of the most powerful men in the world, became embroiled in a sexual relationship with Lewinsky that nearly cost him his presidency. Clinton's willingness to engage in the affair and subsequently lie about it under oath led to a national scandal that resulted in his impeachment by the House of Representatives for perjury and obstruction of justice. While Clinton remained in office, his political legacy was forever tarnished, and the scandal haunted him throughout the remainder of his career. Lewinsky, though young and initially enamored by the power and prestige of the president, became a pawn in a much larger political game. Clinton, driven by his direct and forceful nature, allowed his desire for Lewinsky to compromise his integrity, judgment, and ultimately his presidency. The scandal showed how even the most powerful men can be undone by their inability to control their desires, falling prey to emotional and physical temptation.

Jeff Bezos and Lauren Sanchez (2019)

Jeff Bezos, the founder of Amazon and one of the richest men in the world, became embroiled in a high-profile scandal when his affair with former TV anchor Lauren Sanchez was exposed in 2019. At the time, Bezos was married to Mackenzie Scott, with whom he had built a life and a fortune. The exposure of his affair came through leaked text messages and photos, leading to a very public divorce that cost Bezos billions of dollars in the settlement. While Lauren Sanchez did not necessarily "manipulate" Bezos in a nefarious sense, the affair and Bezos's obsession with her became a significant distraction, pulling him into a whirlwind of media scrutiny and personal turmoil. His marriage, one of the longest among the billionaire elite, fell apart, and he lost a considerable amount of wealth and public goodwill. This example highlights how even the wealthiest and most powerful men, driven by their desires, can make decisions that compromise their personal and professional lives. The consequences of the affair extended beyond financial losses, damaging Bezos's image and leaving him vulnerable to public and media attacks.

Johnny Depp and Amber Heard (2016–2022)

The tumultuous relationship between actor Johnny Depp and actress Amber Heard resulted in one of the most publicized and toxic legal battles in recent history. Depp, one of Hollywood's most iconic actors, became embroiled in a series of lawsuits with Heard following their divorce, with both accusing the other of abuse and manipulation. Depp, initially captivated by Heard, allowed his infatuation to pull him into a relationship that quickly spiraled out of control. The relationship, marked by accusations of violence, drug use, and emotional manipulation, severely damaged Depp's career. He lost major acting roles, including his iconic part in the "Pirates of the Caribbean" franchise, and faced a massive public relations crisis. Heard, for her part, used allegations of abuse to gain public sympathy, further escalating the damage to Depp's career and reputation. Though Depp ultimately won a defamation lawsuit against Heard in 2022, the years-long battle took a significant toll on his finances, career, and mental health. Depp's involvement with Heard, driven by his initial obsession and emotional investment, serves as a modern example of how a powerful man can be brought down by a toxic relationship, losing both status and wealth.

Rupert Murdoch and Wendi Deng (1999–2013)

Media mogul Rupert Murdoch, one of the most powerful and influential businessmen in the world, became entangled in a marriage with Wendi Deng, a former intern at one of his companies, in 1999. Deng, 38 years his junior, was known for her intelligence and social connections. Throughout their marriage, she exerted considerable influence over Murdoch, positioning herself as a central figure in his media empire. However, their relationship soured amid rumors of Deng's closeness with other powerful men, including former British Prime Minister Tony Blair. When Murdoch filed for divorce in 2013, it was widely speculated that Deng's ambition and strategic relationships had played a key role in the dissolution of their marriage. Deng's influence over Murdoch during their marriage was significant, as she used her position to secure financial and social standing for herself. Murdoch's decision to marry Deng, driven in part by his attraction to her youthful energy and ambition, ultimately led to a highly publicized divorce that cost him both personally and professionally. Deng walked away with significant assets and influence, while Murdoch's personal life was laid bare before the media.

Elliot Spitzer and Ashley Dupré (2008)

Elliot Spitzer, the former governor of New York, was forced to resign in 2008 after it was revealed that he had been involved in a prostitution scandal with high-end escort Ashley Dupré. Spitzer, known as a fierce prosecutor of financial crimes and corruption, became a victim of his own hubris when his secret life of paying for sex came to light. Spitzer's obsession with Dupré and his willingness to risk his political career for his indulgences exemplifies how powerful men can be easily manipulated by the allure of a toxic relationship. His public disgrace ended his political career and exposed him to ridicule and scorn. Dupré, on the other hand, capitalized on the media attention, gaining notoriety and eventually launching a career in music and business.

The SUM

What good is being able to rule a kingdom, run a company, lead/coach a winning team if we allow a seemingly harmless looking creature to destroy us in a flash. Throughout history, men of great power—whether through obsession, love, or lust—have fallen victim to the manipulative charms of women who used their influence for personal gain or political leverage. Whether through direct manipulation or the subtleties of emotional and psychological influence, these women capitalized on the vulnerabilities of powerful men, often leading to their downfall. From Cleopatra and Delilah to Anne Boleyn and Madame de Pompadour, these historical examples illustrate the timeless dynamic where men's forceful nature is often outmaneuvered by the indirect and strategic approaches of women. One fact remains very clear; They are fully Intune with their powers and abilities, and we can get or stay Intune long enough to recognize the subtle changes in our environment when it comes to intimate encounters. You are not lesser than...in fact we (men) are the true prize. Without our seed...the world (as far as human population goes) stops growing. The matter of fact is we need discipline more than ever if we hope to survive this next evolution of human progression. The phrase "Adapt or Die" has never resonated more than now in this modern era. In the modern era, just as in ancient times, powerful men have been brought down by their inability to control their desires and their vulnerability to manipulative or toxic relationships. From political leaders to billionaires and actors, the stories of these men serve as a reminder that obsession and infatuation can blind even the most successful individuals, leading to personal and professional ruin. The lesson for today's men, particularly in the MONETIZED dating market, is to recognize the power dynamics at play and to approach relationships with a level of emotional intelligence and self-awareness that prevents them from being manipulated or losing control of their lives.

03 |

THE FALSE PROMISE OF FINANCIAL INDEPENDENCE

Fantasy vs Reality

I n the modern dating market, some women have figured out a way to capitalize on men's primal instincts and monetize themselves, not just for survival but to maximize their leverage based on men's physical desires. The truth is, a woman today can charge anywhere from $200 to $500 an hour for her time, leveraging her body as a commodity to gain quick returns. On paper, that might seem like a smart hustle, but here's where the trap sets in: while the earning potential is massive, it's not consistent enough, and the psychological and physical demands eventually take their toll. Many women in this game, even those who rake in big bucks short-term, end up broke and living hand to mouth. You see, they may have short bursts of high income, but the long-term stability just isn't there. The real issue? It's not just the money; it's the mindset. The hustle is temporary, and without a clear plan or sense of teamwork, they burn out fast. They're operating solo, often missing the bigger picture of how to build long-term wealth and stability. They focus on immediate gain, failing to create a foundation that could lead to lasting success. Now, here's the irony: women are often labeled as "natural nurturers" – beings who supposedly excel in building harmony and working together. But in today's market, many miss the mark when it comes to true partnership. Instead of building alongside a man, they see him as a target to exploit for a quick financial hit. That's not harmony; that's short-sightedness. Real power doesn't come from transactional interactions; it comes from collaboration, strategy, and knowing how to leverage long-term. True wealth is built when both parties work in sync, creating a solid foundation, rather than feeding into short-term desires for temporary satisfaction. In the end, the grind of monetizing oneself this way is unsustainable. The physical strain and the psychological drain of constantly selling the illusion of desire wear down even the toughest. These women may control the game for a while, but without a long-term strategy for financial freedom, the hustle becomes just another trap.

The psychological toll of women monetizing their physical desirability in the modern dating market is well-documented in various studies. While the short-term financial rewards might seem appealing, the long-term consequences often paint a different picture, highlighting emotional, mental, and physical decline. Let's break it down with supporting research and psychological insights.

1. Emotional and Mental Exhaustion

Women who engage in commodifying themselves often face deep emotional exhaustion. This stems from the necessity of constantly performing a persona that meets societal expectations of beauty and desirability. According to a study published in Psychology of Women Quarterly, women who rely on their physical appearance for economic gain are more likely to experience emotional dissonance. This happens when there's a disconnect between the person they portray and who they truly are. Over time, the effort required to maintain this "performance" can lead to burnout, anxiety, and depression. The constant need to please and attract can leave them feeling hollow, as their sense of self-worth becomes tied to external validation. Additionally, these women are often objectified, which according to objectification theory, reduces their sense of personal agency and leads to negative psychological outcomes. When a person becomes the object of another's desire, they are reduced to nothing more than a vessel for fulfilling someone else's needs, which over time can erode their self-esteem and lead to a fragmented sense of identity.

2. Lack of Long-Term Stability and Life Satisfaction

Research has shown that the pursuit of short-term financial rewards at the cost of personal well-being leads to a cycle of instability. A study in The Journal of Sex Research found that women engaged in transactional relationships or sex work often report higher levels of financial insecurity in the long term. This is primarily because their income is inconsistent and unsustainable. While some may earn significant amounts in brief periods, the absence of a solid financial plan or investment strategy often leads to financial mismanagement and, eventually, poverty. This lifestyle also leads to lower levels of life satisfaction. According to Maslow's Hierarchy of Needs, humans seek fulfillment beyond the base level of survival. While money might meet immediate physiological and security needs, the lack of deeper emotional connections and a sense of purpose leads to dissatisfaction. Women who monetize themselves often lack meaningful relationships built on mutual respect and trust, which are critical for emotional fulfillment and well-being.

3. The Physical Toll

The physical demands of constantly maintaining an attractive appearance can be staggering. Women who commodify themselves often engage in extreme measures to stay competitive in the market, from cosmetic surgeries to rigorous dieting and exercise routines. Over time, this obsession with physical perfection can lead to body dysmorphia, eating disorders, and other health-related issues, according to a study in The International Journal of Eating Disorders. Moreover, the physical aspects of selling one's body, whether through escorting, sugaring, or even in a digital sense (e.g., OnlyFans), often result in a deterioration of personal health. The pressure to always be "on," combined with the need to meet clients' or followers' demands, creates a stress cycle that negatively impacts physical well-being. Chronic stress, as supported by research from the American Psychological Association (APA), can weaken the immune system, disrupt sleep patterns, and increase the risk of serious health problems like cardiovascular disease.

4. Psychological Impact of Objectification

A key concept in literature is self-objectification. When women engage in selling their desirability, they may begin to see themselves as objects rather than whole human beings. This internalization can lead to severe mental health issues, including depression, anxiety, and a diminished sense of self-worth. A landmark study in The Journal of Personality and Social Psychology concluded that women who self-objectify often experience lower cognitive functioning and a greater propensity toward mental health problems. This is compounded by the fact that many of these women face dehumanizing treatment from the men they engage with. Research from The British Journal of Social Psychology highlights how the transactional nature of these interactions can strip women of their personal agency, reducing them to commodities whose value is based solely on their appearance and ability to please men. Over time, this can lead to profound psychological distress, including feelings of isolation, worthlessness, and disconnection from their authentic selves.

5. The Cycle of Shame and Guilt

A 2019 study published in Sexuality & Culture found that many women in the monetized dating market experience deep feelings of shame and guilt over time. Despite the initial financial benefits, they may feel conflicted about the lifestyle they've chosen, leading to internalized shame. This is particularly true for women who were raised with traditional values or those who struggle with societal judgment. This guilt can manifest in self-destructive behaviors, further eroding their sense of self-worth and making it difficult to escape the cycle. As time goes on, the internal battle between maintaining the facade of empowerment and dealing with the reality of emotional emptiness grows stronger. A study in The Journal of Feminist Studies in Religion points out that women often mask their vulnerabilities behind a veil of confidence and independence, when they are battling deep-seated insecurities and shame related to their lifestyle choices.

The SUM

While the modern dating market offers some women the opportunity to quickly monetize their desirability, the long-term psychological, emotional, and physical costs are substantial. Many women may see this as a path to financial independence, but the inconsistency of the earnings combined with the mental toll creates a volatile situation. Without the ability to form meaningful partnerships, develop emotional resilience, or plan, the lifestyle becomes unsustainable, leading to burnout, financial instability, and a diminished sense of self. The key takeaway is this: while short-term financial gain might seem empowering, the real leverage comes from building something sustainable and meaningful. The grind is not just about what you can get today; it's about positioning yourself for long-term success— financially, emotionally, and mentally. A transactional lifestyle lacks the depth and partnership needed to build real wealth and happiness, and many women ultimately pay a steep price for chasing short-term gain at the expense of long-term fulfillment.

04 |

THE CHEAT CODE FOR MEN

Retention, Fasting, Clean Diet, and Regular
Exercise

In the pursuit of personal growth, self-discipline, and peak performance, many men are turning to a holistic approach that combines retention, fasting, a clean diet, and regular exercise. Together, these practices form a powerful synergy that can enhance mental clarity, emotional stability, and physical health. Let's break down how each component contributes to the overall cheat code for men, supported by psychological literature and resources. First things first, you must realize that exercise is the Foundation of Physical and Mental Strength. Building physical strength is like setting a foundation for every challenge that life throws your way. Regular exercise isn't just about muscles or appearance; it's about creating a mindset of discipline, resilience, and mental clarity that's essential for navigating the inevitable trials men often face—divorce, alimony, financial burdens, and the emotional strain that follows. You see, when you commit to a consistent exercise regimen, you're not just transforming your body; you're fortifying your mind. Consider exercise to be your armor in this long battle. Physical fitness directly boosts your stamina and energy levels, which means you're not just prepared to handle the everyday stresses of life but ready to tackle the unexpected. Research consistently shows that men who engage in regular physical activity have lower levels of cortisol, the stress hormone, which skyrockets during high-stress periods like divorces and legal battles. Being physically fit puts you in a better position to withstand both the physical and psychological demands of these situations. (Hassmen et al., 2000) When a man is fit, he has options. If the pressure in one location becomes unbearable or job demands require extra hours, having a body that's conditioned for endurance gives you the flexibility to adapt. I touch on this subject in my other book "Blue collar Ballin: The playbook for industrial athletes". You can move quickly, adapt to new environments, and keep pace with demands without succumbing to fatigue. It's like putting yourself in the driver's seat, even when the road gets rough. When you're in peak physical condition, you can pivot and make life decisions that serve your best interests. Beyond the physical, exercise cultivates mental resilience, a critical asset for handling high-stakes situations. Studies show that regular exercise stimulates the release of endorphins and neurotransmitters like dopamine, which improve mood and combat symptoms of depression and anxiety. For men dealing with emotional strain—whether from relationship challenges, financial burdens, or parental responsibilities—staying physically active is a powerful countermeasure. (Paluska & Schwenk, 2000) Think of each workout as a test of your ability to overcome discomfort and push past perceived limits. That same grit is essential when navigating emotional upheavals.

When your mind is conditioned to handle the physical demands of lifting weights or running miles, it translates to a stronger mental ability to handle stress and anxiety outside of the gym. This kind of resilience can make the difference between succumbing to stress and emerging stronger and more composed through life's trials. We must remain Prepared for Life's "Rough Patches". Every man knows that life will throw curveballs, and one of the biggest sources of stress often comes from relationship challenges. Divorce, custody battles, or financial struggles can drain you mentally, emotionally, and financially. By investing in your physical health, you're setting yourself up to handle these challenges head-on. Physical fitness isn't just about strength; it's about survival, about ensuring that you're prepared to fight for yourself and your future no matter what obstacles stand in your way. A man who's healthy and fit has the stamina to endure long legal battles, the discipline to stay productive during tough times, and the resilience to bounce back from setbacks. Exercise becomes a form of self-defense, a necessary practice that empowers you to maintain control over your life's narrative, regardless of the outside pressures. When you're in peak shape, the burden feels lighter because your body and mind are conditioned to carry it.

Benefits of Staying Physically Fit

- **Work Flexibility:** A strong, healthy body ensures you can take on additional work or side jobs if you're strapped financially.

- **Resilience:** Divorce can trigger severe mental and emotional stress. Exercise, healthy eating, and regular self-care keep your mind sharp and your body resilient.

- **Leverage in Custody Battles:** If you're in great shape and living a healthy lifestyle, it demonstrates to the court that you're a responsible and fit parent, giving you a better shot at custody or visitation rights.

Psychological Benefits

- **Increased Self-Esteem and Confidence:** Exercise is strongly linked to improved self-esteem. A study published in Health Psychology found that regular physical activity boosts body image and confidence, which can be particularly beneficial for men looking to assert their masculinity and personal power.

- **Enhanced Mood and Reduced Anxiety:** Physical activity stimulates the release of endorphins, known as "feel-good" hormones. Research from the Journal of Clinical Psychiatry shows that regular exercise can significantly reduce symptoms of anxiety and depression, contributing to improved emotional well-being.

- **Practical Application:** Incorporating regular exercise into a daily routine fosters a sense of discipline and accomplishment. Men who prioritize physical fitness often experience enhanced mood, increased energy levels, and improved mental clarity, all of which are crucial for pursuing their goals.

The SUM

Regular exercise is more than a routine; it's a tool of empowerment. It strengthens your body and your mind, providing the foundation you need to thrive in good times and survive in the tough ones. When you commit to your physical health, you're not just investing in muscle; you're building a reserve of strength, resilience, and mental clarity that will see you through life's inevitable rough patches. In a world that's constantly testing your endurance, physical fitness is your constant. It's the base from which you can pivot, adapt, and overcome. It keeps you in control, prepared, and ready for anything—whether that's moving for a new job, handling financial strain, or simply managing the psychological weight of life's challenges. So, suit up, get strong, and stay ready, because real strength comes from knowing you're prepared for anything. Semen retention isn't a magic solution, but it is a powerful tool in the arsenal of a disciplined man. It's about making the conscious choice to direct your energy towards goals that matter—building wealth, improving your health, and expanding your knowledge. It's about realizing that every ounce of energy you retain is fuel for your vision. You're not just saving your energy; you're investing it in your future. In the end, this practice is about becoming the best version of yourself. You're not just denying yourself pleasure; you're cultivating focus, mental clarity, and resilience. This is how you achieve real power and success—not by chasing, but by building. The women and the rewards will always be there. But if you let your time slip away chasing things that bring only temporary satisfaction, you'll lose the chance to reach your full potential. Remember, the grind waits for no one. Time is finite. It's up to you how you choose to use it. When you understand the biological cost of each release, semen retention becomes more than just an abstract idea, it's a choice to invest in yourself. Instead of spending what's valuable, you're saving it up for when it really matters.

Semen Retention: Practical Patience is more than a virtue

Your time and energy are finite, and every choice you make contributes to the man you're becoming. Preserve your strength, channel your energy, and let the results speak for themselves. Focus on building, not waste. Retention, often referred to as sexual retention or semen retention, involves abstaining from ejaculation to redirect sexual energy into other pursuits. This practice is rooted in various ancient traditions, including Taoism and certain yogic practices, and has gained modern attention for its potential benefits. Let's get real: the pursuit of sex and the non-stop indulgence in quick gratification— whether through casual encounters or the endless rabbit hole of porn—is draining men of their true potential. Every time you let your focus and energy get lost in the pursuit of the next high, you're giving away something more valuable than you realize: your life force, your creative power, your drive. Semen retention isn't just about holding back; it's about taking back control of your mind and using your energy to build something tangible and real. For thousands of years, ancient practices like Taoism and yoga understood the significance of preserving this energy. It's not some outdated philosophy but rather a blueprint for those who aim to be stronger, sharper, and more purpose driven. Semen retention is about creating focus. It's not just about what you're saying "no" to but what you're saying "yes" to—a focused vision, financial growth, skill mastery, and ultimately, the respect that comes with self-discipline.

The Trap of Over-Pursuit:
Sex, Porn, and Their Toll on the Male Brain

We live in a society that encourages men to constantly chase the next thrill, particularly when it comes to women and instant pleasure. But think about it: what happens every time you indulge? You're rewiring your brain to expect instant gratification. Studies show that watching porn floods the brain with dopamine—the "reward" chemical. This flood of dopamine over time makes it harder for you to find satisfaction in anything else. That's why men get stuck in cycles, craving the next hit just like any addict would. Every time you release, your energy level drops. This isn't just a theory; science backs it up. Studies have shown that men experience a spike in testosterone after periods of abstinence. Testosterone fuels your ambition, strength, and willpower. When you're constantly spending that energy, you're depleting the very fuel that drives success. You're left weaker, physically and mentally, without the energy to pursue meaningful goals. Instead, you're in a loop of distraction, and over time, it becomes a habit that's hard to break. Semen retention isn't just about abstinence; it's about redirecting that energy. The purpose is what gives it power. When you commit to this practice, you're not just resisting temptation; you're channeling that desire into something greater. It's the ultimate form of self-control. Instead of letting that energy go to waste, you're using it to fuel your ambition, drive, and productivity. This energy, when redirected, empowers you to focus on personal growth, skill-building, and wealth generation.

Think of it like this: when you stop wasting your time chasing superficial heights, you suddenly have more time to grind, learn, and execute. Men throughout history have used this technique to maximize their potential. Nikola Tesla, for example, claimed that he refrained from relationships to focus entirely on his work, and ended up creating inventions that changed the world. That's the kind of power we're talking about. You've got a finite amount of time to make your mark—don't waste it chasing temporary highs when you could be building an empire. Men in general need a major Mindset Shift because contrary to popular opinion, "Women and Sex Aren't Going Anywhere". Men often feel this urgency to chase women as if the opportunity will somehow disappear. But here's the truth: women and sex aren't going anywhere. The chase is always going to be there, but your time, your youth, and your prime years are ticking away. By practicing semen retention, you're putting yourself in the driver's seat. You're saying, "I control my life. I'm not a slave to my impulses." You're making the decision to be on your grind instead of letting distractions pull you off course. There's something powerful about a man who's focused on his purpose. People respect that energy. And ironically, when you're not chasing, that's when real opportunities present themselves. When you've built something, when you're strong in your mind and body, the women you attract will be on a whole different level. You're not coming from a place of neediness but from a place of strength. And by the time you're ready to engage, you're in control, not being driven by desperation or validation. When it comes to semen retention, it's essential to understand what's at stake with every release. Each ejaculation isn't just a physical activity, it's a biological transaction. Your body invests high-value resources to create semen. Each time you release, you're letting go of a cocktail of nutrients, vitamins, and minerals that your body could otherwise use to fuel your strength, resilience, and focus. This isn't some vague idea; it's backed by science.

The Nutritional Cost of Ejaculation: What's Lost Each Time

Studies show that ejaculation involves a loss of vital nutrients, including zinc, magnesium, calcium, potassium, and amino acids. These are the building blocks of muscle recovery, mental focus, and immune strength. Zinc, for example, is one of the most critical nutrients for men. It's involved in everything from testosterone production to immune function. Each ejaculation depletes a notable amount of zinc, which directly impacts your energy levels, mood stability, and physical endurance. Think about that—every time you release, you're spending your body's reserves of zinc, and it's not easy to replace. In fact, some studies suggest that semen is rich in over 200 proteins, as well as vitamin C, vitamin B12, and vitamin E. Vitamin B12 is crucial for mental focus and energy, while vitamin E plays a role in cardiovascular health. So, with every release, you're pulling from a reservoir that powers you physically, mentally, and emotionally. Zinc Depletion is indeed a low-key Silent Killer of Male Vitality.

Zinc isn't just an optional nutrient; it's foundational for male strength. Low zinc levels have been shown to lower testosterone, weaken the immune system, and lead to chronic fatigue. Men who constantly release without replenishing can experience a downward spiral of energy, drive, and mental sharpness. The effects are cumulative. You might not notice the impact immediately, but over time, your body's reserves get depleted, leaving you weaker, both in stamina and in mental resilience. The last thing a man needs in this world is brain fog, especially considering the amount of opposition waiting for us all outside. Be mindful of the other essential elements lost to reckless sexual behavior's such as: Magnesium, Calcium, and Potassium: The Backbone of Strength and Stability. Magnesium is a critical mineral that's lost with every release. Magnesium is known as the "anti-stress" mineral because it calms the nervous system, supports muscle relaxation, and helps regulate sleep. Without it, stress and anxiety increase, and physical recovery suffers. Calcium and potassium play roles in muscular function and heart health, as well as bone density. Regular release means you're shedding off these elements that contribute to maintaining physical stability and resilience over the long haul. You also lose Amino Acids and Proteins which are The Blueprint of Recovery. Amino acids are the building blocks of protein, essential for muscle repair and growth. Semen contains a range of these amino acids, including L-arginine and L-carnitine. L-arginine is known for improving blood flow and supporting cardiovascular health. When you're constantly depleting your reserves, your ability to build and repair muscle weakens. So, every time you ejaculate, you're stripping away the resources that your body relies on to stay physically strong and ready to face challenges head-on. Everything has a consequence, and the over pursuit of instant sexual gratification has Cumulative Effects when it comes to Constant male Release. All these nutrients are like the "currency" of your body's internal bank. When you're constantly withdrawing without making deposits, you're left with an energy deficit. You feel it in your stamina, mental clarity, and overtime, even in your mood. The practice of Semen retention allows you to maintain that energy, to keep those resources within you, fueling everything you do—from pushing through a tough workout, creating that new business plan, to staying mentally sharp during critical tasks. Realigning Your Energy for Growth and Purpose is the new base for this ongoing war we're currently involved in. The goal here isn't to suppress your desires but to use your energy more wisely. By holding onto your resources, you're giving yourself the fuel to level up physically, mentally, and spiritually. This practice is about more than just abstinence; it's about realigning your focus and giving your body what it needs to build strength and resilience. Imagine putting all that energy and focus into your hustle, your personal development, and your growth. Instead of being drained, you're continuously charging up.

Psychological Benefits

- **Increased Focus and Motivation:** Research suggests that abstaining from sexual activity can lead to increased levels of dopamine and testosterone, which are linked to motivation and focus. A study published in Neuroscience Letters found that a temporary increase in testosterone levels can enhance cognitive performance.

- **Emotional Stability:** Retention can lead to improved emotional regulation. According to The Journal of Positive Psychology, individuals who practice self-control in one area (like sexual restraint) often experience a spillover effect, enhancing self-regulation in other areas of life.

- **Practical Application:** Men who engage in retention report heightened energy levels, better concentration, and a stronger drive to pursue their goals. By focusing their energy inward, they can channel it toward personal and professional achievements.

Fasting: Mental Clarity and Resilience

Fasting, the practice of intentionally abstaining from food for specific intervals has been valued across cultures for its health and spiritual benefits. Today, more men are recognizing that fasting isn't just about shedding pounds—it's a training ground for mental resilience, discipline, and focus. When a man commits to fasting, he's doing more than just abstaining from food; he's teaching his mind and body the power of self-control, a trait that translates far beyond diet alone. Through the temporary sacrifice of immediate satisfaction, fasting gives a man an edge in self-mastery, clearing his mental fog and sharpening his sense of purpose. Train and Tame Impulses through the Mental Clarity provided via Fasting: The act of fasting pushes you to confront impulses head-on. For hours or even days, you're deliberately holding off from immediate satisfaction. Research in neuroscience shows that fasting activates the brain's prefrontal cortex, the area responsible for decision-making, focus, and impulse control. By practicing restraint with food, you're exercising this mental muscle, teaching yourself to overcome the immediate pull of cravings and act with intent rather than reaction. This newfound clarity goes beyond just resisting food; it extends to resisting distractions and temptations that can pull you away from your goals. For example, fasting has been shown to increase the production of brain-derived neurotrophic factors (BDNF), a protein linked to cognitive function, memory, and neuroplasticity. With higher BDNF levels, your brain operates on a sharper level, helping you focus better and think more clearly, even under pressure. This focus is essential for men who want to redirect their energy from the distractions of today's dating market to achieving self-defined goals.

Fasting can also help in Redirecting Desires, thus Curbing the Urge to Chase. When you learn to go without food for a while, something interesting happens: the constant craving for instant gratification, in all its forms, starts to lose its power. Men often talk about how fasting allows them to refocus, putting time and energy back into pursuits that matter. With this discipline comes a reduced need for external validation, like chasing temporary relationships or blowing money on transactional dating. The modern dating market thrives on a man's impulses—pay-to-play models, casual flings, and "monetized" connections that drain energy and resources without adding long-term value. Fasting, in its essence, teaches a man that he doesn't need to give in to every impulse. In the same way that you're saying "no" to a meal for the benefit of physical health, you can say "no" to superficial dating dynamics that demand time and money but give nothing back. Remember gentlemen, this is a war, so Psychological and Spiritual Resilience is indeed key. Research has also shown that fasting can increase dopamine levels, enhancing mood and motivation over time. Unlike the fleeting highs of external pursuits, dopamine generated through fasting is tied to a sense of accomplishment, resilience, and inner peace. This is the type of dopamine boost that can keep a man focused on his path, avoiding the energy-draining chase of temporary gratification. Many religions and spiritual practices have long promoted fasting to achieve higher levels of self-awareness and spiritual resilience. By abstaining, one cultivates an appreciation for what truly matters, turning inward rather than reaching outward. In a world where men are constantly pressured to keep up with superficial standards, fasting can be a powerful grounding tool, redirecting focus to personal growth over social status or false validation.

Financial Gains and the Discipline Dividend

There's an undeniable financial advantage to learning restraint through fasting. By honing this skill, a man cultivates a mindset that values long-term wealth and stability over fleeting indulgences. This restraint can naturally carry over into finances; rather than spending hard-earned money on dating expenses or superficial luxuries, a disciplined man focuses on investments, skills, and future-building endeavors. The money saved from not "feeding" every dating impulse can be channeled into wealth-generating assets, creating financial freedom and long-term security. Consider a man who uses the mental clarity gained through fasting to restructure his finances or take on new skills that multiply his income. This strategic approach creates a foundation for generational wealth, positioning him as an example of strength and foresight for his children, who are likely to adopt the same disciplined habits.

Ultimately, fasting builds an unbreakable core. It equips a man with the focus, discipline, and mental clarity to act intentionally in all areas of his life. By learning to control his physical appetite, he strengthens his control over his desires in the larger, more complex world, freeing himself from dependence on superficial validation or transactional relationships. Instead of being swayed by the pressures of the monetized dating market, he operates from a place of inner strength and clarity.

Psychological Benefits

- **Enhanced Cognitive Function:** Studies have shown that fasting can lead to improved cognitive function and clarity. Research published in The American Journal of Clinical Nutrition suggests that intermittent fasting can boost brain-derived neurotrophic factor (BDNF), which plays a crucial role in learning and memory.

- **Increased Resilience:** Fasting teaches discipline and resilience. According to Health Psychology Review, individuals who practice fasting often report greater self-control and mental toughness, as they learn to cope with hunger and cravings, which can translate into other areas of their lives.

- **Practical Application:** Incorporating intermittent fasting into one's lifestyle can lead to improved mental clarity, better decision-making, and an enhanced ability to stay focused on long-term goals without being distracted by immediate gratification.

Clean Diet: Fueling Body and Mind

A clean diet emphasizes whole, unprocessed foods, including fruits, vegetables, lean proteins, and healthy fats. This dietary approach not only fuels the body but also supports mental and emotional well-being. When it comes to showing up at your best, what you're putting into your body matters. A clean diet isn't about looking good on a calorie count or just hitting the gym with some protein bars. It's about fueling yourself with purpose, with intention, and setting up the foundation for every move you make. When you're focused on eating whole, unprocessed foods—real stuff like lean meats, fresh veggies, whole grains, and healthy fats—you're setting yourself up for strength that lasts, energy that doesn't crash, and a mental edge you can rely on.

You are what you eat; there's no way around it. You want to be strong, to build muscle, to have energy that doesn't give out halfway through the day. That doesn't come from a fast-food diet or empty calories that taste good for five minutes and leave you dragging or lethargic for hours. Real strength? That comes from fueling your body right. Lean proteins like chicken, fish, and fresh vegetables aren't just filling you up, they're rebuilding every fiber of your muscles. And complex carbs like oats, sweet potatoes (yams), or quinoa? They give you the kind of steady energy that keeps you going strong. Then there are the healthy fats—avocado, olive oil, nuts—that keep your brain and body sharp. Don't sleep on this. If you're eating with purpose, you're setting yourself up to move through life with the kind of power that people notice. You've got energy on tap. You've got strength you can call on anytime. And that's what a clean diet gives you—sustainable power that lasts if you need it. What you eat affects how you think and feel, and anyone telling you different is lying. A clean diet isn't just about physical gain; it's about mental and emotional gain, too. Studies show that foods rich in omega-3s (from things like fatty fish, walnuts, and flaxseeds) help keep your brain sharp, your mood stable, and even prevent cognitive decline. When you're eating clean, you're choosing mental clarity over fog, focus over distraction. Fruits, vegetables, whole foods, they're not just fueling your body, they're supporting your mental resilience and keeping you steady in a world that tries to knock you down. To be blunt, we all should strive to eliminate or at least Stay Away from Processed Junk as much as possible. Processed foods are cheap thrills—short-term highs with long-term damage. They give you that rush of energy, but it's followed by a crash that leaves you weaker than before. Sugar spikes? They're only going to make you feel foggy, distracted, and drained. Those "convenience" foods are robbing you of the energy you need to get real work done. What's more, they create inflammation in your body that can mess with your gut—and your gut is directly connected to your brain. So, every time you reach for something that's been processed, you're risking more than just weight gain. You're risking the sharpness and discipline that keeps you in control. Discipline in the Kitchen equals Discipline in Life, and that the ism...When you commit to eating clean, you're doing more than following a diet; you're building discipline. You're proving to yourself, meal by meal, that you're in control. This isn't just about skipping the junk food or choosing salad over fries—it's about establishing habits that reinforce your power over yourself. The discipline you build through a clean diet translates into every area of your life. When you can control what you put into your body, you show yourself that you can control your mind, your habits, and ultimately, your future.

Clean Diet Over Dating:
Prioritizing health in a Monetized Market

In today's monetized dating landscape, where nearly every interaction carries a price tag, and STI rates are spiking like never before, a man must make choices that serve his highest good. It's not just about cutting through the noise; it's about establishing priorities that set you up for the long game. When you're truly dialed in, putting time and energy into a clean diet and health-focused habits, the need to chase validation in the form of relationships fades. Instead, you're building a foundation of power—physically, mentally, financially—that keeps you on top no matter what comes your way. It's a fact: the energy and focus you invest in a clean diet directly translate into gains you won't get chasing fleeting satisfaction. For one, a clean diet elevates your energy levels, which means you're performing at peak capacity across all areas. If you're running on whole, unprocessed foods, your stamina, both mental and physical, is unmatched. Compare that to the highs and lows that come with the drama of today's dating scene. Sure, there's the thrill of the chase, but it's often followed by an energy crash—emotional drain, financial expense, and exposure to unnecessary risks.

The SUM

A clean diet is more than just "healthy eating"—it's living with intent. It's saying no to the shortcuts and empty calories and saying yes to the long game. It's about setting yourself up with the kind of energy, strength, and mental clarity that fuels every area of your life. It's about showing up with purpose, day after day, and knowing that you're taking care of yourself from the inside out. So, make the choice. Choose foods that strengthen you, that fuel you, that keep your mind clear and your energy steady. Embrace the discipline that a clean diet requires and let it empower you to build the life you're grinding for. Because when you're intentional about what goes into your body, everything else falls in line. And that's when you're unstoppable.

The monetized dating market has transformed relationships into transactions. and the risk? It's not just financial. According to recent CDC data, STI rates in the U.S. have surged, with gonorrhea, syphilis, and chlamydia hitting all-time highs in recent years. Particularly in high-risk dating pools, these rates show no sign of slowing down. The dating scene has evolved into a marketplace where surface-level engagement and quick encounters are more common, leading to increased health risks that can derail you mentally and physically. Consider this: by sticking to your health goals— investing in a clean diet, fitness, and the discipline that comes with them— you're creating a natural barrier against unnecessary exposure to the risks of the dating market. The result is more stability, fewer distractions, and a stronger foundation to build wealth, knowledge, and a legacy. When you focus on self-care over casual dating, you're not just avoiding health risks; you're safeguarding your energy, resources, and clarity. A clean diet isn't just about what you eat; it's a lifestyle that supports long-term goals. It's about building resilience and maintaining clarity in a society that values instant gratification. While the dating market pushes the notion of casual encounters and monetized affection, a clean diet and disciplined health habits remind you of your higher purpose. You're operating in a world that rewards delayed gratification, investing in the things that will last—your health, your mind, and your mission. The benefits of a clean diet go far beyond physical health; they touch on mental resilience, which is critical for navigating the pressures of today's world. Studies show that individuals who maintain a clean, nutrient-rich diet experience reduced levels of anxiety, depression, and mental fog—common effects of today's overstimulated, transactional dating culture. Consuming whole foods rich in omega-3s, B vitamins, and antioxidants has been shown to enhance mental clarity and reduce mood fluctuations, giving you a sharper edge for decision-making. With heightened mental resilience, you're better equipped to focus on your personal growth, professional ambitions, and life goals, without the distraction of constantly seeking validation in relationships.

Case in Point: The Athlete's Mindset

Take high-level athletes as an example. Their lifestyle revolves around health and discipline. For them, clean eating isn't a diet; it's a way of life that fuels every aspect of their journey. When you adopt that mindset, you're not interested in superficial distractions. You're working with precision, choosing to elevate your life through choices that compound over time. That's not to say relationships are off the table. It's about holding out for connections that align with your standards and purpose, rather than falling into the time-consuming, often draining cycle of modern dating.

The SUM

In this current era, where dating is just as transactional as any business deal, investing in a clean diet is a power move. It's a testament to your commitment to self-mastery, health, and longevity. By prioritizing your well-being, you're opting out of a system designed to drain your resources, energy, and focus. Instead, you're building a strong foundation that will serve you in every area of life, from career to legacy to real, meaningful relationships down the line. So, the choice is clear: stay on the path of discipline, fuel your body and mind with purpose, and keep building a life where every decision serves your highest goals. When you commit to a clean diet over casual dating, you're making a declaration: that your journey, your purpose, and your self-worth are not up for grabs. You're in control, and that's the real definition of power.

Psychological Benefits

- **Improved Mood and Energy Levels:** Research in Nutrients indicates that a balanced diet rich in nutrients can have a positive impact on mood and cognitive function. Nutritional deficiencies can lead to fatigue and irritability, while nutrient-dense foods can enhance energy and overall well-being.

- **Reduced Anxiety and Stress:** A clean diet is associated with lower levels of anxiety and stress. According to a study in The American Journal of Psychiatry, diets high in fruits, vegetables, and omega-3 fatty acids are linked to lower rates of depression and anxiety.

- **Practical Application:** Eating a clean diet empowers men to maintain steady energy levels throughout the day, supporting both physical activity and mental focus. When men fuel their bodies with nutritious foods, they are better equipped to tackle challenges and maintain high performance.

The Synergy of Practices: A Holistic Approach to Success

The combination of retention, fasting, a clean diet, and regular exercise creates a powerful synergy that amplifies the benefits of each individual practice. Together, they help men cultivate discipline, enhance mental clarity, and promote emotional stability. Here's how they work in harmony:

- **Enhanced Energy Levels:** Retention and a clean diet boost energy, while fasting and regular exercise optimize how that energy is used.

- **Improved Focus and Clarity:** Each practice contributes to sharper mental acuity, helping men stay on track with their goals and ambitions.

- **Resilience and Discipline:** The challenges presented by fasting, retention, and physical training foster a resilient mindset that translates into other areas of life.

Always Remain focused on Unlocking Potential Through Discipline. For men looking to elevate their lives, adopting these four practices—retention, fasting, a clean diet, and regular exercise—acts as a cheat code. Supported by psychological literature, these strategies cultivate self-discipline, enhance mental clarity, and foster emotional stability. By prioritizing these holistic approaches, men can unlock their full potential and become the best versions of themselves, ready to tackle any challenge that comes their way. The modern dating market, especially in its monetized form, is full of distractions, illusions, and traps designed to pull men away from their purpose. But for the man who stays focused on his goals and remains clear-headed about the dynamics at play, there is a long-term payoff that far outweighs the short-term allure of engaging in the dating circus. While many women monetize themselves based on physical desirability and fleeting interactions, the man who chooses to avoid the noise and focus on self-development is setting himself up to become the ultimate prize—a man of value, purpose, and wealth.

The Value of Walking Your Path

The man on his purpose understands that his time, energy, and resources are precious. He's not wasting hours chasing women who see him only to an end. Instead, he's focused on building his empire, honing his skills, and developing his financial, physical, and mental prowess. This man isn't moved by fleeting trends or short-lived gratification. He plays the long game, knowing that success requires discipline and sacrifice. Research on goal-oriented behavior shows that men who stay focused on their long-term objectives—whether it's career advancement, financial independence, or personal development— achieve greater life satisfaction. A study published in The Journal of Positive Psychology found that men who prioritize their goals over distractions tend to experience higher levels of self-esteem and long-term well-being. Meanwhile, the woman who chooses to monetize herself in the short term, exploiting men's desires, is ultimately bound for a path of diminishing returns. While she may experience bursts of financial gain, the inconsistency of that lifestyle, combined with the mental and physical toll, often leads to burnout and financial instability. Over time, her value in the dating market decreases as youth and beauty fade, leaving her scrambling to maintain relevance. In contrast, the man who stays on his grind only becomes more valuable with time.

Men Increase Value Over Time

The modern world is structured in such a way that men, when they invest in themselves early, become more attractive as they age. Unlike women who often monetize their physical appeal, men's value is rooted in their accomplishments, their wealth, their wisdom, and their status. A man in his 30s or 40s, who has built his career and maintained his health, becomes the highly sought-after prize—especially by women who begin to realize that their youthful charm no longer holds the same leverage. Psychological studies support the notion that as men mature, their perceived value in the dating market increases. A report from Evolutionary Psychology found that women tend to be drawn to men with resources, status, and stability—traits that often develop later in life. While the impulsive, unfocused man who spends his younger years chasing after fleeting pleasures finds himself depleted, the man who has stayed disciplined becomes the embodiment of what many women ultimately seek. As women face the inevitable realities of the dating market—where their value is often front-loaded and declines with time— they become increasingly drawn to men who are stable, financially successful, and mentally sharp. This puts the focused man in a position of power, having developed not only his wealth but also his discernment. He's no longer impressed by superficial displays of beauty or seduction; he's looking for true partnership, if he even chooses to entertain it at all. Remain present and mindful of your surroundings to Avoid the Pitfalls of the Modern Dating Circus. The man who remains focused on his purpose sidesteps the drama, emotional manipulation, and financial exploitation that often come with engaging in the modern dating market. While many men fall into the trap of seeking validation through women, getting caught up in their charms and spending valuable time and resources, the man on his grind understands that his mission is bigger than momentary pleasures.

In today's dating economy, many women are not just looking for love—they're looking for a transaction. They're monetizing their looks, their time, and their attention, and men who lack focus are the ones paying the price. But for the man who remains centered on his own growth, the benefits are twofold: he avoids financial exploitation, and he strengthens his mental fortitude by not being swayed by external distractions. According to The Psychology of Money by Morgan Housel, men who practice delayed gratification and remain disciplined in their financial and personal growth efforts tend to amass greater wealth and fulfillment in the long term. This principle applies directly to dating as well. While men who chase after short-term pleasures lose focus and resources, the man who invests in his future eventually finds himself in a position of immense value. The harsh reality is that many women who prioritize monetizing their desirability over building long-term skills or partnerships end up trapped in a cycle of diminishing returns. Their short-term strategy may provide some financial gains, but it often comes at the cost of emotional well-being, self-respect, and future security. As youth fades and competition increases, these women find it harder to maintain their lifestyle, often leading to desperation or poor decisions down the line. In contrast, the man who chooses to ignore this circus of temporary gratification is steadily building an empire. He's not concerned with the immediate approval of women, nor is he chasing after fleeting desires. Instead, he's creating a life where he controls his destiny—financially, physically, and mentally. By the time he reaches his peak, he's not the one chasing; he's being pursued. Women who once monetized themselves will look at this man as the ultimate prize, because he offers something they can no longer buy with just beauty or seduction: stability, power, and success. In essence, while they were chasing short-term financial gain, he was building long-term wealth and value. Leverage and peaceful negotiation are the Ultimate Reward for the Focused Man. The focused man, the one who stays on his purpose, eventually reaps the rewards of his discipline. As he rises in status, wealth, and influence, he becomes the embodiment of success. The women who once ignored him for flashier, short-term gains now view him as the goal. But here's the twist: by the time he reaches this level, he's in control of his destiny. He's no longer the one being manipulated or led astray by external forces. He calls the shots. In the grand scheme of things, staying focused on your purpose ensures that you avoid the pitfalls of the modern dating market, which is full of illusions and traps designed to derail your progress. By focusing on building your empire—whether it's through financial success, personal growth, or intellectual development—you position yourself as a man of immense value. While many women who relied on their physical appeal find themselves struggling as they age, the man who remained steadfast on his path is the one who ultimately wins. He becomes the prize. The lesson is simple: stay focused on your purpose, because while the women who chase short-term gain are destined for destruction, the man who builds his life with purpose and intention will always come out on top. In the end, he becomes the one who is highly sought after, not just for his wealth or status, but for his unwavering dedication to success.

05 |

UNDERSTANDING THE DYNAMICS
Men's Desires vs. Women's Needs

I n the modern dating landscape, it's essential to understand the underlying motivations that drive men and women in their interactions. Men are often motivated by two primary desires: the pursuit of pleasure and the drive for legacy through reproduction. Women, on the other hand, are frequently focused on securing resources for survival and stability. Understanding these fundamental differences is key to navigating the modern dating market effectively.

Men's Dual Desires: Pleasure and Legacy

Theres no secret that Men seek Pleasure as a means of release and relaxation: The Pursuit of Physical Satisfaction At the heart of many men's motivations is the desire for physical pleasure—namely, sexual experiences. This biological drive is deeply rooted in evolutionary psychology. Men are wired to seek out partners who provide sexual gratification, which can often lead to impulsive behaviors in the dating market. The thrill of pursuing pleasure can cloud judgment, causing men to overlook red flags or engage with women who may not align with their long-term goals. Everyone knows this all too well by now, so why do men remain victims of circumstance? Here's some Psychological Insight for those in the back with excessive ear wax. Research in evolutionary psychology posits that men's attraction to physical beauty is not just about aesthetics; it's also tied to reproductive potential. Men are often drawn to women who exhibit signs of fertility, consciously or unconsciously seeking to maximize their chances of reproductive success. This desire for physical intimacy can sometimes lead men to engage in short-term relationships that may not contribute to their overall goals. In other words, my G; "Learn of move through life from a counterintuitive perspective. Clearly utilizing the straightforward approach to dating and courtship will lead to your destruction. You must realize by now who amongst the sexes give a daman about the state of world and or the future which men refer to as Legacy. The Drive for Reproduction The second driving force behind men's desires is the instinct to leave a legacy—often expressed through reproduction. This desire for immortality manifests in the quest to pass on genes and create a family. In today's context, this translates to seeking meaningful connections with women who can be potential partners in this endeavor. Of course, under the eclipse of modern dating, legacy seeking is designed to make you a target for the darker side of feminine nature.

Make no mistake...a woman will put her body through the rigors of a nine-month pregnancy just to slave out her male counterpart of the rest of his life if she gains enough leverage. Hers some Psychological Insight for the penguin mindset type males: According to The Journal of Personality and Social Psychology, men often derive a sense of self-worth from their ability to provide and protect. This drive for legacy shapes their preferences in partner selection, leading them to seek women who can contribute to a stable family environment. Men who prioritize these goals tend to cultivate long-term relationships, enhancing their chances of achieving both pleasure and legacy. Mind you, being focus and on purpose helps your overall "chances", it doesn't hold any real sway on the universal outcome. You must find a female that truly matches your energy and respects your ambitions. Those two traits are rapidly falling by the wayside unfortunately.

Women's Needs: Resources and Stability

First things first, you better realize female nature is Survival and self-preservation. The Pursuit of Security In contrast, women are often driven by the need for security and stability. In evolutionary terms, women have historically sought out partners who can provide resources—whether emotional, financial, or physical. This desire is rooted in the instinct for survival, as women with access to resources are better positioned to raise offspring successfully. Psychological Insight: Research published in Evolutionary Psychology indicates that women prioritize partners with traits that signal the ability to provide—such as financial stability, ambition, and social status. This drive influences women's choices in the dating market, often leading them to prioritize long-term partnerships over short-term flings. In the modern context, women may seek out men who exhibit these traits to secure their future and that of their potential children. The Challenge of the Modern Dating Market While these motivations are rooted in biology and psychology, the modern dating landscape presents challenges for both men and women. Men pursuing pleasure may find themselves entangled in relationships that do not serve their long-term goals (only short-term physical needs being met), while women seeking resources may encounter men who are less interested in commitment, i.e., Men are realizing it's a total wash trying to commit to a woman that can and most certainly will leave you once the successful gestation period has occurred. This disconnect can lead to misunderstandings and dissatisfaction on both sides. You must realize you're in a constant battle, and war with a deadly creature hardwired for survival (1st). We are witnessing the first era of female brutal honesty in recorded history in terms of mating, dating, courtship and marriage. Men love women, and women love what men can do for them often. Ussery is at an all-time high in the west at the time of me writing this book. The feminist movement has effectively removed the mask off traditional monogamy, with women openly admitting to using men for resources, time, energy, and attention. Vampires of the modern age, only this variety doesn't burn under sunlight, garlic won't repel them, they still perform best under the cover of night or the cover of darkness.

Navigating the Divide: Strategies for Success

For Men: Focus on you own Purpose and Value To successfully navigate the modern dating market successfully, men should also prioritize their long-term goals (First). By focusing on personal development, career advancement, and emotional intelligence, men can cultivate their value and attract women who are seeking stable, committed partners later along the journey, and only once such a man aligns his goals and ambitions, otherwise the broke-simp existence awaits. As stated in previous chapters, Retention and Discipline should be a staple in your life moving forward. By engaging in practices such as semen retention (SR) can help a man redirect their energy toward achieving their goals, making them more appealing as partners do to the male resetting his senses, self-esteem, and sexual energy. Building Wealth and Stability are also put front and center, but why!? Some may ask. By focusing on financial stability and career growth, men position themselves as attractive partners who can provide the security women often seek, even though we get to the bag for ourselves and our own benefit first n foremost. Women will say one thing and often do another thing in the same vein, so it's important to pay attention to a woman's behavior, more readily than her words all the time. They'll say they're Seeking Compatibility and Stability but lack any clarity in their desires. By understanding their need for resources and stability, a man can make more informed decisions about their potential partners, by simply viewing them for what they are without judgment. When Assessing Compatibility in the arena, Men should prioritize development of their own emotional intelligence to gain mutual respect in relationships, by ensuring that their partners align with their long-term goals from the Avoiding of Short-Term Gains. By resisting the allure of superficial relationships, men can focus on building connections, and a viable network that offer genuine stability and support. Plant the seed of The Long-Term Vision, i.e., Building

Meaningful Relationships, but Ultimately, remember, the key to success in the modern dating market lies in recognizing and respecting the differences in motivations between men and women. By understanding that men seek pleasure and legacy (initial mode of operation) while women seek resources and stability (initial mode of operation), both can navigate the dating landscape more effectively. Men must take the initiative by Fostering Mutual Understanding, while navigating this evolved relationship landscape. Encouraging open communication about desires and expectations can bridge the gap between these motivations between both genders. Both men and women should strive to create environments where they can express their needs honestly, leading to healthier, more fulfilling relationships. Just don't let your ideal scenario blind you to the ongoing battle you're now fighting in. Creating a balanced lifestyle is key for men focusing on their purpose and value, so participate in the dating market, just always remain mindful that women prioritize stability and resources over attraction and love. Men should work towards building meaningful partnerships that satisfy their fundamental desires while keeping your leverage and options intact. In doing so, they can transcend the pitfalls of the modern dating circus and create legacies that align with their aspirations by choosing carefully who to invite into their personal space.

The SUM

Mastering the Modern Dating Market by understanding the dynamics of men's desires and women's needs, individuals can better navigate the complexities of the modern dating market. Men who remain focused on their purpose and build value while women prioritize stability, and emotional intelligence can create partnerships that fulfill both parties' needs. This approach not only fosters lasting connections but also enhances the potential for mutual growth and success. Ultimately, embracing this understanding is the key to thriving in the contemporary dating landscape.

06 |
THE FINANCIAL FALLOUT OF DIVORCE
The monetized Man

I n the modern dating landscape, understanding the potential financial consequences of divorce is crucial for men. When relationships dissolve, particularly marriages, the cost can be staggering. Men often find themselves on the losing end of divorce settlements, not only in terms of emotional distress but also significant financial losses. This section explores the average costs of divorce for men, focusing on the impact on assets, money, and investments, and why a man on his purpose should be cautious about entering long-term commitments without foresight. I never knew just how valuable I was until I filed for Divorce from my Ex-wife. Don't get my words twisted, I was very aware that I was making significant progress in life, as by then I had already amassed a net worth of 2.1 million dollars via stock and crypto based investments by 2020. Twelve years of grinding in my aerospace career, stock trading, starting a merch business, a podcast, and writing 3 books I was riding high and still am, but in the eyes of the family court, I looked like a 18 year meal-ticket via a federal law called (Title IV-D). The law is part of the Social Security Act of 1975. Title IV-D establishes a partnership between the state and federal government to provide child support services. In other words, it's a mafia-based law as it paints the government as the provider and the father or ex-husband as the funder. The MOB i.e., the government/state effectively replaces the father and functions as an enforcer or pseudo "Nazi SS" organization that will violate the father in the even he doesn't adhere to the lopsided guideline layout during mediation or trial. This is one of the many reasons the ex-spouse (the mothers) act so bold.

The Real Direct Costs of Divorce: Legal Fees and Court Expenses

Many Men still need to gain an understanding of the "Average Cost of Legal Fees". Divorce can quickly become a costly legal battle, especially if contested. On average, men can expect to spend between $15,000 to $30,000 on legal fees alone. High-conflict divorces involving disputes over children, alimony, or asset division can drive these costs much higher. Then you'll come to the Mediation vs. Litigation crossroad. In some cases, mediation can reduce costs. In the best cases you'll have options for Mediation in the form of a free option which most certainly works against you because you get what you pay for, and then you have the paid option where you hired a mediator (usually a close business associate of the firm, remember everyone eats of the man's body at the time of divorce. However, litigation, which involves a prolonged court battle, can significantly increase expenses, particularly when both parties refuse to compromise.

Don't forget the Psychological Impact on you, the family on both sides, as people are forced to empathize usually with the relative as opposed to the spouse. The financial strain of these legal fees adds to the psychological burden of divorce. Studies from The American Journal of Family Therapy indicate that the stress of legal costs contributes to increased anxiety and depression among men, further complicating the recovery process after a divorce. You might not want to admit this to yourself or speak this out loud, but young men especially need to prepare for the rug-pull attack that most certainly is on the table of every relationship.

Division of Assets: Losing What You've Built

Property and Real Estate: One of the biggest financial hits men face during a divorce is the division of property and real estate. If a man owns a home, car, or other substantial assets, these are often split, with the wife typically receiving a significant portion. This is the reason why all men, especially younger men should spend their 20's building themselves, in the pursuit of tangible leverage for the future. Establishing yourself prior to a female entering your space is critical for self-defense later. You should never aim to live off another person's resources, especially a woman's resources, as the narrative will immediately be turned against the man in a negative way. Yes, you will be called selfish, yes beta-cuck type males will verbally assault you, yes woman will call your sexuality into question the second you choose not to be an automatic provider. Any bashing experience should roll off you, like water rolls off a duck's backside. Real Estate Losses: In many states, assets acquired during the marriage are considered "community property," meaning they must be divided equally. For example, if a man owns a home valued at $500,000, he may be required to sell the property and split the proceeds, or buy out his spouse's share, which can lead to financial strain or even the loss of the home. This is why you should avoid living with a woman and most certainly avoid moving in with her. Investment Portfolios and Retirement Funds are another significant financial loss involve retirement accounts (401(k)s, IRAs, pensions) and investments. Divorce courts frequently award a portion of a man's retirement savings to his ex-spouse through a Qualified Domestic Relations Order (QDRO), which mandates the division of these funds. Investment Divisions are also put on the table as well. For example, if a man has accumulated an investment portfolio worth $200,000, he may lose anywhere from 30% to 50%, depending on state laws and the nature of the settlement. This loss can severely impact his financial future, especially if these investments were intended for long-term growth and retirement. The you have, Alimony and Child Support, which for men who earn significantly more than their spouse, alimony (spousal support) can become a long-term financial obligation depending on the settlement. On average, alimony can range from $1,000 to $5,000 per month, depending on the duration of the marriage, the income disparity, and the lifestyle maintained during the marriage. Of course, you may have to wrestle with the Alimony Duration as a man. In many cases, men are required to pay alimony for years or even decades, sometimes until their ex-spouse remarries. In high-income situations, this can amount to millions over the course of a lifetime.

See my G, the system is setup for men to inevitably take a fall in the end. They set it up so that the woman gains a pseudo manservant without having to give him anything in return. Last on the list is Child Support, which means for men with children, child support is another financial burden. The average child support payment in the U.S. is about $500 per child per month, but this number increases based on income, and if there are multiple children, the costs compound. Over 18 years, this can amount to $108,000 per child, or more. Now imagine if the mother took that money and invested it, because many will claim the amount of money they receive little or large amount is "not enough".

Let's do the rough math scenario based on a realistic situation. Let's say for the sake of argument a man and woman never got divorced and simply decided to set aside a nest egg for their two children. These two parents decide to set aside 800.00 per child into a custodial ROTH IRA effectively making a $1600.00 investment monthly over the course of th3 standard 21-year age that people famously think makes you a mature adult at least in the western world. To calculate the future value of a Roth IRA investment of $1,600 per month for 21 years with compounding interest, we need to make some assumptions about the annual rate of return. Assuming an average annual return of 7% (historically speaking), which is a reasonable long-term estimate for stock market investments, the formula for future value with monthly contributions is:

$$FV = P \times \frac{{(1 + r/n)^{nt} - 1}}{{r/n}} \times (1 + r/n)$$

Where:

- The monthly investment (**$1,600**)

- The annual rate of return (**0.07**)

- The number of times the interest is compounded per year (**12 for monthly contributions**)

- The number of years (**21**)

- After investing $1,600 per month into a Roth IRA for 21 years at a 7% annual return, the total value of the investment would be approximately **$918,892.44** (pretty much a million dollars (USD)) due to compounding.

Instead of setting your children up to be future millionaires so they can start life fresh and ripe with opportunities, our landscape has been compromised with faulty foundational floors, bait n switch tactics, extreme feminists' ideology, and a disregard for the future (children) in general. Women are truly in business, while men unfortunately remain in-love.

Emotional Costs:
How Divorce Drains More Than Finances

Divorce not only hits a man's wallet but also affects his mental health and well-being. The financial stress of losing assets, income, and investments can lead to a downward spiral in motivation and focus. Mental Health Strain is a hidden foe man many never defeat post-divorce. Psychological literature, including studies from the Journal of Men's Health, shows that men often suffer from higher rates of depression, anxiety, and even suicidal ideation post-divorce, largely due to financial strain and loss of identity. The emotional toll of losing not just money but also access to children, property, and social standing can lead to a prolonged period of recovery. Let me be the first to admit, this is most certainly a true thing many men go through, me included, even though I'm the one that filed in my case. Any momentum you have halts, but it's more like watching a freight train attempting a full stop with tons of cargo hooked up. The heavy metal will slide for miles before the brakes finally take over and gain an upper hand. You find yourself asking yourself questions like...was I attentive enough, did I ask the right questions, did I show enough interest etc....Then you have to deal with the public ridicule that comes with a divorce, usually by people with zero skin in the game in terms of being married, living with a woman for a prolonged period of time, and actually living live with another on the teamwork side of the house. It's easy to say how to rearrange furniture, it's a whole other animal to lift and move a heavy couch or a piano into a new position. You'll get the typical societal man bashing statements such as: "maybe he(you) was hitting right!"(even though she let herself go in front of you, and denied any sexual advances from you", "She has every right to leave" (especially after she had your children (her new leverage, you foolishly gave her), "Go Get your money up"(Even though she just crippled you financially thanks to the family court system.), "choose better next time"(even though it takes years to truly get to know someone, especially in any intimate way.) All this will slowly rip, and tear your self-confidence as a man, no matter how self-conscious and self-assured you normally are, this situation will cause self-doubt, self-esteem issues, and cause you to reflect, retool, and recalibrate yourself into a new being. The men without a support system, and outlet, or a reason to smile end up falling deeper into depression, going from a rut to a grave in no time.

Long-Term Impact: Recovering from Financial Losses

Rebuilding Finances Post-Divorce for many men, can take years, if not decades (10 years on average), to financially recover from a divorce. According to Forbes, men often experience a 40% decrease in their net worth post-divorce. This decline is compounded if alimony and child support obligations extend over many years. This is why you must think and live a builder type lifestyle with a Boss-up mindset, so that you can recover from any punch you don't see coming. Getting discipline, saving, investing, and creating multiple income sources independent of the W-2 path. The notion of retirement is still on the table, must remain constant for you my G.

You cannot let the enemy beat you into submission. Maybe you had plans to retire at 40, now you went through this divorce in your late 20's- early 30's. Congrats, as you now have the rest of your life to find out what makes you tick in new ways, you get to travel, you get to study new things, gain new experiences etc. Many of the bro's will say, but I must work and kill myself for her benefit, what about the kids, what about the other dude she's fucking and sucking. To that I say who cares. You were going to work anyways, you're no longer with her. You were going to hold your kids down regardless because you're a great father, so Be there as much as possible and make sure whenever your children do see you, spend time with you, or interact with you, they see and experience you winning in life. She (They) wants war...I say wipe your tears (because nobody really cares) and give her the battle of her life. Make the mom hold up her life against the backdrop of yours and let society and the children choose and draw a comparison, because that is what's inevitably going to happen at the end of the day when the smoke clears and everyone's of an older age. Delayed Retirement is on the table during such life impacting events as One of the most damaging impacts is the effect on retirement plans. Men who lose a portion of their retirement savings and investments may have to work several more years than originally planned, delaying their ability to retire comfortably, but it's not a death sentence, as long as you draw breath you have time to get it right. Which brings me to the stage of Rebuilding Wealth, where Men who successfully recover financially post-divorce often do so by adopting aggressive saving and investing strategies as I stated, thus reducing their expenses overtime, and, in some cases, rebuilding their careers or starting over in a new industry. Take this event as a wakeup call to action. Maybe she tried you because your weak, maybe she shits tested you to near death because you had zero leverage to dangle in her face. She dragged you because in her eyes you couldn't or wouldn't bounce back effectively. You owe it to yourself to boss-up despite the deliberate takedown attempt and attempted subjugation of your manhood by a well-funded and incentivized system. This is the time to reinvent yourself, to do all those things you put on the back burner out of some strange inclination to protect your spouse's feelings or views. You want to pick up that new skill (go learn it), you want to read up a new subject of interest (read it), you want to instill and impute your brand of life knowledge into your children without being undermined in front of them (no you have the stage my G).

Remember, you, me, or any other man is no good to anyone in our bubble of influence if were not constantly improving ourselves. Yes, you'll grow older, yes, your body won't respond the same way that did once did when you were a younger male, but that's why we all should aspire to attain coach status. We can still play the game of life, on a high level but leveling up must remain our mantra of life especially during a post-divorce situation.

Benefits of a Focused Man on His Purpose

Do everything in your power to Avoid the Dating Circus. For men who remain focused on their purpose—building wealth, achieving career success, and prioritizing self-development— typical financial pitfalls of divorce can be avoided. A man who prioritizes his life mission and avoids being distracted by the modern dating circus often finds himself in a far better position long term. No late nights wasting time lurking in a random female social media DM. No more dating while your bank account is empty, as this gives off a desperate energy signature to all that encounter its vibe. Instead, you should focus on Building Value. Men who focus on building their value over time— financially, mentally, and physically—become highly sought after in the marketplace, both in business and relationships. This is due to the man creating a gap or space of separation between them and every other man competing. By staying disciplined and avoiding impulsive decisions, they position themselves for greater success. All men in fact should be stoic as they remain locked-on to the true prize. Wishing, or waiting for her to hit the wall or Face Decline is weakness and a waste of creative energy. In contrast, many modern women who monetize their beauty and sexuality for short-term gains may find themselves in a precarious position as they age, but that is none of your business. We all know, just like time knows...no matter what, they'll all lose the ability to leverage physical attraction for financial resources, they know this is finite, and once that fade, many women who failed to build long-term stability face financial difficulties. These types are some of your harshest critics, as they've crossed passed the jaded threshold into the barren wasteland of bitterness. Understand this my "G" ...she (they) could care less for the pain or stress of others, and that's a formula for Destruction. The modern woman who relies solely on her physical attributes for leverage often misses out on opportunities for real financial growth, peace, and stability. As a result, while a man who stayed focused on his goals continues to build wealth and value, she may find herself in a vulnerable position later in life, struggling to maintain her lifestyle, but that won't be you, and that's the bottom line. This is not heartless rhetoric, this is a mirror mainly being reflected on men, however this is a chess match and war tactics must be implemented.

Divorce: The Real Cost and the Power of Focus

For men, the financial consequences of divorce can be devastating—leading to significant losses in assets, investments, and long-term wealth. However, men who remain focused on their purpose and avoid the pitfalls of impulsive relationships can safeguard themselves from these outcomes. Playing defense should always be in the forefront of your mind when you're navigating this new dating space. By building value, wealth, and stability over time, prior to dating, the disciplined man can navigate the modern dating market without falling prey to the financial and emotional costs of possible divorce. Ultimately, the man who focuses on his mission becomes the highly sought-after prize(later), while those who get caught up in the dating circus chasing instant gratification often face financial destruction. The term "dishwasher family court calculator" refers to the idea of how family courts, particularly in Western countries, calculate financial responsibilities like alimony (spousal support) and child support, often leading to men feeling "washed out" financially after a divorce. This metaphor hints at how these calculations, despite being formula-based, can seem to drain men's financial resources, much like dishes going through a relentless cycle of being washed. Let's break down how family courts typically calculate these obligations and why the results often feel disproportionate from a man's perspective.

Alimony (Spousal Support) Calculation

Alimony is designed to support a lower-earning spouse, allowing them to maintain a lifestyle like what was established during the marriage. (She gets to leverage your resources without having to talk or see you on any level, effectively making the ex-husband into a long-term wage slave. Courts use a variety of factors to determine alimony payments, which can feel arbitrary or unfair depending on the situation.

Key Factors in Alimony Calculation

- **Income-Disparity:** The primary basis for alimony is the difference in income between the two spouses. Courts assess the earning potential of both parties. If the husband earns significantly more, he is typically required to support the spouse or the lower-earning spouse.

- **Length of Marriage:** Longer marriages often result in larger or longer-lasting alimony payments. A 20-year marriage, for example, can lead to lifetime alimony, whereas shorter marriages might only require temporary support.

- **Standard of Living:** The court considers the lifestyle established during marriage and seeks to ensure that the lower-earning spouse can maintain it post-divorce. This means that if the couple lived in a wealthy, high-spending lifestyle, alimony payments are calculated to support that same lifestyle for the spouse, even after the divorce.

Common Alimony Formula

In many states, alimony is determined by a percentage of the difference in income. For instance, a standard alimony formula might be 30% of the higher-earning spouse's income minus 20% of the lower-earning spouse's income. This results in a monthly payment to help balance financial inequality.

Hypothetical Example

- Husband earns $100,000 per year.

- Wife earns $30,000 per year.

Applying the formula

30% of $100,000 = $30,000

20% of $30,000 = $6,000

Alimony = $30,000 - $6,000 = $24,000 per year, or $2,000 per month.

Long-Term Impact on Men

Men who are the primary earners often find that a significant portion of their post-divorce income is tied up in alimony payments. This, combined with other financial obligations like child support, can severely limit their ability to recover financially, save for retirement, or rebuild their lives. Not only knowing about the system designed to destroy you...but accepting it entirely is the first step all men on purpose should do, end of the day.

Child Support Calculation

Child support is designed to ensure that children maintain the same standard of living after the parents' divorce. Like alimony, it's calculated based on the income of both parents (but you will be held to 100% account especially if you decided to be a sucker for love and provide a stay-at-home landscape for your wife to thrive), but with specific attention to the needs of the children.

Key Factors in Child Support Calculation

- **Parental Income:** Both parents' incomes are considered, but the higher-earning parent often shoulders a larger financial responsibility.

- **Custody Arrangements:** The amount of time the children spend with each parent affects the calculation. A parent with primary custody typically receives child support payments.

- **State Guidelines:** Each state has its own child support guidelines, which dictate the percentage of income that must be paid based on the number of children.

Child Support Formula

In many states, a standard formula calculates child support based on a percentage of the paying parent's income. For example, a father might be required to pay 20% of his income for one child, with the percentage increasing for each additional child.

Hypothetical Example

- Father earns $80,000 per year.

- The state mandates 20% for one child.

- Child support = $16,000 per year, or $1,333 per month.

Deeper Impact on Men

When child support payments are combined with alimony, many men find that upwards of 40-50% of their income goes toward supporting their ex-spouse and children, leaving little room for personal financial recovery. This scenario can push men to work extra jobs, limit their ability to invest in their future, or, in some cases, fall behind on payments, leading to legal penalties.

How the System Feels Stacked: **The "Dishwasher" Effect**

The term "dishwasher" speaks to how men feel like they're being put through an endless financial cycle. **Here's why:** Fixed Payments, and Variable Income as the court calculations don't account for fluctuations in the payer's income. For instance, if a man loses his job or experiences a downturn in income, alimony and child support payments remain fixed unless he petitions the court for modification, which can be a lengthy and expensive process. In other words, the father (the male) held to a different standard than the mother(female). You must work, or at least consistently generate income, zero questions asked, or you are threatened with extra court fees due to violations, not to mention the threat of imprisonment due to lack of payment. As a man this seem demoralizing, because your character and role as a father has been placed into a tight box under lock and key, held by the family court system ("the mother mafia"). You need to know about the Imbalance in Lifestyle that takes place generally post-divorce. The court's intention to ensure that both parties maintain a similar lifestyle often leaves the higher-earning spouse, typically the man, living at a much lower standard than they did while married. They are often forced to downsize, delay retirement, or take on additional jobs to make ends meet while supporting their ex-spouse and children. Funny how there's so many independent women walking around living or should I say leveraging the income and resources of another person while stacking their own is a very potent mix for controlling a societal narrative. Then you must deal with any possible Long-Term Financial Drain that takes place.

Many men are tied to these payments for years, sometimes even decades, depending on the length of the marriage and the number of children involved. By the time these payments end, they may have little in savings and face a delayed financial recovery dependent on the age of divorce. Since many men don't get married and make life-long commitments with the intention of ending the commitment abruptly for no reason other than temporary boredom and emotional instability. The Psychological Toll is something that gets swept under the rug on all accounts by many, especially women and the family court system. The financial burden of being trapped in the system, particularly if the man feels that the payments are disproportionate, can lead to severe mental health issues. The feeling of being constantly drained, with no end in sight, mimics the cyclical nature of dishwasher-cleansing, only to start the process over again with each paycheck. This emotional strain is well-documented in studies on the effects of financial stress post-divorce. Divorce doesn't just leave a man heartbroken; it can break his mind, his finances, and even his will to live. The numbers don't lie, as divorced men are roughly 2.5 times more likely to commit suicide than married men. Why? It's deeper than just losing a relationship—men often lose their sense of purpose, their identity, and the emotional support they never knew they relied on so heavily. Men don't build networks like women do, and when a marriage ends, that social and emotional isolation hits like a truck. Psychologically, men have been conditioned to "man up" and suppress their feelings. So, when divorce rips their lives apart, they have nowhere to turn. A Journal of Epidemiology study found that this isolation is a major factor behind the mental health decline of divorced men. They lose more than just their wives; they lose the person they emotionally depended on, whether they knew it or not. Let's talk about the financial toll. Divorce courts don't play fair (everyone knows this fact). In fact, the system often leaves men strapped for cash with alimony, child support, and divided assets. Research by sociologist Edward Kruk revealed that men often suffer more financially post-divorce, with women more likely to gain custody and associated benefits. This financial wreckage compounds the mental burden, leaving men feeling like failures—both as providers and protectors. The financial strain becomes an emotional strain, making them feel like they've been stripped of everything they worked for. This isn't just anecdotal Rant—it's backed by the data. The CDC reports that men account for nearly 80% of all suicides in the U.S., with divorced or separated men being a significant part of that statistic. When you tie in the economic and emotional devastation, it's clear why these men feel hopeless. Their identity was wrapped up in their role as a husband, father, or provider, and divorce can feel like a complete undoing of their purpose. Divorce puts men on the edge, but here's the real message: it doesn't have to be this way. You must start moving differently. Prepare for the worst, protect your assets, stay physically and emotionally sharp, and know the game. The system isn't built for you to win, but if you understand that, you can strategize to avoid being another statistic. This is where mental toughness, emotional intelligence, and strategic planning come into play—your life depends on it.

Financial Strategies to Mitigate the Impact

While the "dishwasher family court calculator" might seem harsh, there are strategies men can use to protect themselves from being washed out by the system...remember, it'

- **Pre-Nuptial Agreements:** One of the best ways to avoid the financial drain of alimony is to establish a pre-nuptial agreement. This legally binding document can outline how assets and income will be divided in the event of a divorce, potentially limiting alimony and asset division.

- **Post-Nuptial Agreements:** For men who are already married, a post-nuptial agreement can offer similar protection, though it may be harder to negotiate.

- **Income Diversification:** Men can protect themselves by diversifying their income streams. By establishing multiple sources of income, they can cushion the financial blow if their primary income is subject to heavy alimony or child support payments. (Side hustles, LLC's, stock trading/Stock dividends, GIG economy jobs for extra income.)

- **Investing in Tax-Advantaged Accounts:** Contributing heavily to tax-advantaged accounts, like 401(k)s and IRAs, Life insurance (Leverage play), or Trust funds (Leverage play) can shield income from being included in alimony or child support calculations, as courts often look at liquid, post-tax earnings.

The SUM: Navigating the Dishwasher

The family court system is designed to create financial equality post-divorce, but for many men, it feels like a never-ending financial rinse cycle. Alimony, child support, and asset division can drain resources, leaving men with less income and limited options for recovery. By understanding the system's mechanics and proactively implementing financial strategies, men can better protect their financial future and avoid being caught in the "dishwasher" cycle of family court calculations. In today's ruthless dating arena, a man who isn't thinking defensively is a man walking into a trap blindfolded. Let's be real— this modern landscape isn't built for men to thrive without strategy. If you're not moving with foresight, you're playing Russian roulette with your life, your money, and your peace of mind. Whether it's a causal relationship, long-term commitment, or marriage, you need to think and act from a defensive, preventative, and insurance standpoint.

The Defensive Mindset

Protecting Yourself Before You Get Played is indeed the mantra of the day. Think of dating and marriage like stepping onto a battlefield. The moment you drop your guard, you're vulnerable, emotional, unstable, and numb to your logical mind, and in this game, that kind of vulnerability costs you everything—your time, your money, your future. You wouldn't walk into a high-stakes situation without a backup plan, so why would you treat relationships any differently? The truth is, modern relationships are transactional, especially modern marriages, and if you don't recognize that, you'll pay the price on the back end. Men have been conditioned to believe in romantic ideals, such as blind faithfulness, and monogamy, but reality says otherwise. In today's world, emotions are fickle, and people switch up quickly. That's why you need to move defensively, making sure you're always protected. It's about being three steps ahead, planning for what "could go wrong" so you can handle it without losing your footing at the time she decides to shake the relationship foundation. Just like your physical health is concerned. Prevention Is Better Than Recovery, which is Why You Must Plan Ahead. They say prevention is better than cure, and that couldn't be truer when it comes to relationships. The most dangerous mistake you can make as a man is believing things will "just work out." They won't. Not unless you take steps to prevent your own downfall. Hard truth is the system isn't built to protect men. I know...I know, big news flash buddy! Divorce courts aren't looking out for your best interests as a man or father, alimony laws are archaic, and custody battles are stacked against you. If you're not actively working to protect yourself from the very beginning, you're already losing. Also, you should always keep Separate Finances, that one flesh garbage only compounds your issues when it comes to splitting assets. Even if she loves you today, feelings change. If all your money is tied up in joint accounts, it can and will vanish overnight. No sense in getting angry after the fact sir...the goal is to never give up that type of leverage. Remember she's counting on you being star struck by her physical assets, a soft skin, her engaging eyes, or her robust smile...all things that don't mean a single thing or hold any real measurable weight in terms of negotiations. The baseline metric for gauging marriage should be Prenuptial Agreements. A prenup isn't just about protecting assets; it's about setting the tone from day one that you're not here to be exploited. Fun fact, if it's truly about loving each other, we shouldn't be talking like it's a business contract. This is what your mother, your aunts, your sisters, female friends/coworkers, and or society in general will ridicule you for... (protecting yourself). It's well on display in the modern dating arena that women are in the relationship for Leverage (business) and the men are in the relationship for love (Legacy). Even more reason for you and me to gain a significant understanding of our state's laws, and or any Legal Knowledge on the subject of family court is concerned. You wouldn't go into business without knowing the risks would you!?, so why do so many men enter relationships clueless about how the law could destroy them? Know the laws, know your rights, and be prepared.

Insurance: The Safety Net When Things Go South

Just like you insure your car, your house, and your health, you need to insure your life against the damage that can come from relationships. And no, I'm not talking about life insurance—I'm talking about life strategy insurance. Insurance means having backup plans and understanding that love doesn't pay the bills or protect your assets. It's about setting yourself up in a way that no matter what happens, you're covered. Utilize Physical Fitness as Insurance also, because health is a form of wealth, and you always want to be able to step back into the arena in top shape. We focus on our health for longevity in life, not just to appeal to the opposite sex. Please understand, if your marriage falls apart, your health shouldn't. Being in peak physical shape gives you the power to pivot suddenly, take on new challenges, and face life head-on without being bogged down by the stress of a relationship collapse, compounded by health issues due to personal neglect on your part. As I stated before in previous chapters, Diversified Income streams are another major key in the defensive stance you must take. You need to have multiple streams of income to weather any storm your significant other unleashes on the household. If you lose half of everything in a divorce, those extra streams can keep you afloat until you get back into a stable groove. Real Estate and Asset Acquisition can give you great leverage in terms of relationship negotiation. Acquire your own property and assets before ringing another into the fold, after all, this will be a good metric to use when comparing where you and any potential mate stack up against each other. The more you have before marriage, the better. And ensure you own it in a way that protects you in case of a split. Property bought before marriage is often off-limit in a divorce, so invest wisely as this Mindset Is Crucial in Today's Vicious Landscape.

The world of dating has changed. Social media, online dating, and a culture that glorifies instant gratification over long-term loyalty have tilted the game. Women have more options than ever, and many have learned to monetize their desirability, turning relationships into business deals. Nothing wrong with them leveraging their physical asset for financial gain, just be mindful that if you're not thinking defensively as a man, you'll be left holding your broken heart and shattered perception while she's moved on to the next conquest. look, this isn't about demonizing women—it's about recognizing the reality of the system and protecting yourself accordingly. Women are conditioned to seek resources and security (predicated on innate survival dynamics), and in this economy, that often comes at a man's expense (because the man is usually the one sought after strictly from a survival perspective. You need to understand this dynamic and position yourself, so you're not left vulnerable when and if things go sideways. I'll even go so far as to say...I don't even think woman want to be monogamous, in fact I don't think they ever wanted to be in the first place. This new technology drive era has shined a bright light on the antics of females, and a in depth look at the modern-day mindset of females thanks to the vanity projector that is social media. So, what's The End Game!?Leverage is the endgame for men, and it must be gained off your own muscle.

Thinking and moving Defensively Makes You the Prize at the end of the day. As a man you're not trying to dominate the opposite sex, but you for sure better make it your mission to never be the one getting taken advantage of by a demon with a beautiful face. Here's the kicker: when you're the man who moves strategically, you become rare and create separation between you and the other beta males vying for female attention (anyway they can attain it). Men who have their assets in order, their health on point, and their finances locked down are highly sought after. You're not just another guy in the mix, you're the guy who has options, who's in control, and who commands respect. Women will notice the difference when you're not the man who can be easily manipulated or blindsided by beauty and charm. When you're focused on your purpose, on building, on protecting what's yours, you become a man that commands respect and admiration, not only from peers, but from the opposite sex…" even if the ladies secretly hate you for exceeding social expectations". You might not be aware of this. But being a successful man comes with its strife, mainly because you reach a level or levels the average person…not just male or female normally never achieve. For example, a typical herd mentality type woman will often call a man lame or boring for always eating clean and exercising, why!? This is due to the fact, most of the low vibrational activities are null in void in that type of man's world (excessive drinking, drug use, prioritizing dopamine hits as opposed to true satisfaction amid accomplishing goals etc.).

As of 2023, the obesity rate for women in the United States is 41.3%, based on the most recent National Health and Nutrition Examination Survey (NHANES) conducted from 2021 to 2023. This survey measures the body mass index (BMI) of adults, and a BMI of 30 or higher classifies an individual as obese. The data shows that obesity is a persistent issue in the U.S., with the prevalence increasing with age. For women aged 40-59, the obesity rate is even higher, at 46.4%. (nearly 50% of woman are obese after age 40) This trend reflects ongoing challenges with public health in terms of diet, physical activity, and overall lifestyle habits, particularly post-pandemic. These are the same females that will attempt to drag a focused man, because he's not focused on them. Instead, they condemn a health-conscious man, because their own health habits are non-existent. When a man has money and money. Those same females will tell that man, he's lame because he didn't always have money, and you should be humble now that you have it and have more options. Men should strive to moderate themselves and activities to achieve balance, as the saying goes "everything in moderation). I noticed this myself during my battle with post-divorce clarity. Balance is the key, and yet eludes so many of us due to excessive, or compulsive behaviors and lack of discipline. Much like the way a college degree represents the discipline, patience, and ability to see goals through to the end, a clean, discipline external life reflects the internal spirit of a man, after all life's a mirror of sorts. Start putting more emphasis on your health and wellbeing, not just killing yourself in the gym for a set of six-pack abs, to appear more attractive to a random woman that has her pick of six-pack abs toting suitors in her rotation. When you put an emphasis on "self-care" as a man naturally unhealthy people (not just unhealthy females) will seemingly vaporize from sight. Gentlemen, seek to vibrate so high that anything lesser than cannot stand in your presence...create a space for natural selection to occur. In this modern jungle, the man with a defensive mindset is the man who thrives. He's not the one getting played, he's the one playing the game—and playing it well. The man who plans, who protects his assets, his time, and his peace of mind, is the one who wins. Every. Single. Time. So, keep your guard up, stay focused, and move smart. Because in the end, you're not just protecting yourself, you're positioning yourself as the prize, and no one can take that away from you. During times of peace..." Prepare for War"

07 |
NAVIGATING THE CHESSBOARD
Impulsion vs. Strategy

Monetized dating isn't just another trend; it's a paradigm shift that forces us to reconsider how we approach relationships. It's not about getting lost in impulsion or diving in for a quick fix. It's about playing the game of life and love like chess—calculated, intentional, and focused on long-term wins. In a world where modern dating is drenched in hidden agendas, monetized dating introduces a different kind of clarity. No beating around the bush, no mixed signals, no endless guessing games. It puts the cards on the table, demanding transparency and authenticity on both sides. As a man, you either step up and approach the interaction with purpose, or you get played. For a man on his grind, this isn't a setback—it's a gift. The transparency here removes distractions and lets you focus on what's worth your time and effort. There's power in knowing exactly where everyone stands from the start. This is the leverage monetized dating gives. Women who engage in this model are upfront about their expectations and values, and that level of honesty can be freeing. You're not left wondering if she's here for the connection, the lifestyle, or the hustle. You know, and that knowledge empowers you to make a choice rooted in clarity. You get to decide what you're willing to give, what you're looking to receive, and how this aligns with your own goals. So many men waste time, money, and emotional energy trying to prove their worth in traditional dating scenarios that hide agendas beneath smiles and charm. But monetized dating changes that narrative. It's not about proving your value;

it's about knowing your value. When the expectations are set, you can move with purpose, knowing you're in control. This new dating economy doesn't just bring clarity; it demands that you set boundaries and adhere to a standard. With monetized dating, your choices are straightforward. You engage in terms of your terms, and you're able to step away when it no longer serves your mission. There's no wasted energy trying to "win her over" in the hopes of a vague payoff down the line. Instead, it's a value exchange, clear and calculated. This is liberating because it frees up mental and emotional bandwidth that you can redirect into building yourself. When you strip away the ambiguity and the games, you gain focus. You get to set terms for how much time and energy you invest. No more pouring yourself into one-sided relationships. This structure allows men to cut through distractions and zero in on their goals. It allows them to approach connections with a strategic mindset, making sure that every move supports the larger picture of self-growth, career, and financial independence.

Strategy over Impulsion: Playing the Long Game

In the monetized dating market, impulsion is your enemy. The men who come out on top here aren't the ones chasing every pretty face—they're the ones operating with strategy. They recognize the value of staying grounded, of not letting short-term thrills throw them off their game. They know that each interaction should add value or at least not detract from their mission. When you approach relationships with a strategic mindset, you're not just reacting to your desires or instincts; you're choosing how each relationship serves your greater purpose. This approach mirrors the discipline needed in other areas of life—finances, fitness, business. You learn to treat every engagement with the same level of forethought you'd bring to an investment. Because that's exactly what it is—an investment of time, energy, and sometimes resources. The key here is to play it like chess. You're not here for impulsive moves. You're here to study the board, make calculated decisions, and ultimately secure a win that aligns with your purpose. The monetized dating market isn't perfect, and it's not for everyone. But for men who want clarity, choice, and focus, it offers an unconventional path that serves as both a litmus test and a playground. It challenges you to stay disciplined, to demand transparency, and to prioritize your purpose. You're not here to be led by impulsion, nor are you here to chase. You're here to choose—with purpose, strategy, and an eye on the future. It's a shift that forces you to grow, to focus, and to use every interaction as another step toward building the life you want. When you approach this market with a strategic mindset, you stop playing checkers with your time and resources. Instead, you're making every move with intention, securing not just a relationship but a foundation that enhances the man you're constantly grinding to become.

1. Brutal Honesty About Recklessness

The era of monetized dating strips away the pretense that often clouds traditional relationships. When women are upfront about their desires— whether it's for a casual encounter, financial support, or simply a good time— men are given an invaluable opportunity to gauge where they fit into that equation. This level of honesty makes it easier for men to:

- **Identify Red Flags:** When a woman openly embraces a reckless lifestyle, it becomes immediately apparent. Men can make informed decisions about whether to engage with her or walk away. There's no need to sift through mixed signals or hidden agendas; the truth is laid bare.

- **Set Boundaries:** The clarity of these transactions allows men to establish their own boundaries. They can engage on their terms, minimizing the emotional fallout that often comes from misunderstandings. If a woman is upfront about her intentions, a man can choose to engage or disengage without guilt or confusion.

2. Sampling Goods Without Commitment

Monetized dating allows men to "sample the goods" for a relatively low cost compared to the emotional and financial investment typically required in traditional relationships. Here's why this is beneficial:

- **No Long-Term Obligations:** Engaging in a transactional relationship means a man isn't saddled with the emotional baggage of long-term commitment. He can enjoy companionship or physical intimacy without the risks that come with deeper emotional entanglements. If things don't work out, he simply moves on, free from the weight of a broken relationship.

- **Quick Satisfaction:** For a fraction of the price of dinner dates, gifts, and other traditional relationship expenses, men can indulge in their desires without the elaborate courtship dance. This efficiency allows men to satisfy their physical needs while staying focused on their personal goals and growth.

3. Time to Grind and Self-Improve

In a society that often pressures men into relationships, monetized dating allows them to reclaim their time and energy:

- **Focus on Personal Goals:** When a man is not invested in a long-term relationship, he can channel his energy into self-improvement, career advancement, and other passions. Without the distraction of managing a complex relationship,

- **Avoiding Emotional Drain:** Traditional relationships can be emotionally taxing, requiring time, attention, and emotional labor. By opting for monetized interactions, men can sidestep the emotional rollercoaster, maintaining their mental clarity and focus on what truly matters in their lives.

4. Empowerment Through Choice

Monetized dating empowers men with choices. Instead of feeling pressured to conform to societal expectations of courtship, they can decide what they want from interactions:

- **Quality Control:** Men can select partners who align with their desires, be it for casual fun or companionship, without the strings attached. This ensures that they're engaging with women who genuinely interest them, making the experience more enjoyable and fulfilling.

- **Fostering a Healthy Mindset:** Knowing that they're not obligated to take care of a woman beyond the transaction helps men maintain a healthier mindset. They can enjoy the experience without the weight of emotional responsibility, leading to a more liberated and self-assured state of being.

- **Acquiring Assets Before Marriage:** One major lesson in the game of marriage is simple: the more assets you acquire before tying the knot, the better. Pre-marital assets are generally considered off-limits in divorce proceedings. By building wealth and investments early on, you protect yourself from losing everything you've worked for during a contentious split.

Types of Pre-Marital Assets to Consider

- **Real Estate:** Owning property before marriage keeps that asset outside of the marital estate in many cases.

- **Investments:** Stocks, bonds, and other securities acquired before marriage are typically not subject to division in a divorce.

- **Business Ownership:** If you own a business (LLC, S-CORP, C-CORP, 501C3 etc.), ensure its well-documented that you were the sole owner before the marriage. This can shield the business from being considered a marital asset.

The SUM: Navigating the New Landscape

In the grand scheme of relationships, monetized dating may seem like a superficial solution to a complex problem. However, for men focused on personal growth and purpose, it offers a unique opportunity to navigate the dating landscape with clarity and intention. By embracing this paradigm, men can enjoy physical intimacy without the emotional traps, reclaim their time for self-improvement, and ultimately position themselves as the prize. While the dynamics of dating may have shifted, men who recognize the advantages of this new approach can thrive. They become more aware of their value, make informed choices, and steer their lives toward success and fulfillment, all while sidestepping the chaos that often accompanies traditional romantic entanglements. So, as the world changes, adapt and leverage these opportunities to stay on top of your game, keeping your focus on what matters most, your purpose and your life.

08 |

THE COST OF COMPLACENCY
Why Lazy, Self-Doubting, and Unskilled Men Will Lose

I n this era of monetized dating and high-stakes choices, there's no room for men who remain complacent, coasting along without a plan, without skills, and without the drive to grow. The reality? This market is ruthless. It rewards those who bring value, discipline, and purpose to the table—and discards those who don't. If you're lazy, if you let self-doubt rule your decisions, if you don't have a single useful skill to show, you're setting yourself up to lose in more ways than one. The days of getting by on potential are over; now, it's all about action, consistency, and showing up with something real to offer. Modern dating demands men who are not only financially stable but also emotionally intelligent and mentally resilient. In a time when options are endless, the pressure to stand out is real, and the consequences of failing to do so are steep. If you're the guy who stays on the couch, doubting yourself, lacking any plan to build or improve, you're effectively handing over the keys to your future to someone else. You're becoming invisible in a landscape that celebrates strength, focus, and commitment. Complacency isn't just a bad habit; it's a poison that seeps into every aspect of your life. A lazy mindset doesn't just stop you from achieving; it slowly erodes your confidence, sabotages your relationships, and limits your earning potential. Each time you choose to sit back and do nothing, you're building a habit that robs you of the life you could be living. Imagine where you could be if you invested that time and energy into learning new skills, mastering financial discipline, or honing your physical and mental strength. Instead, complacency has you stuck in a loop of mediocrity, watching as others pull ahead while you fall further behind. Self-doubt is the enemy of progress, and it's one of the most dangerous forms of complacency. It convinces you that you're not good enough, that you don't deserve better, that there's no point in trying because you'll fail anyway. But here's the thing—every man who's achieved greatness had doubts. The difference is, they didn't let it stop them. They acknowledged fear, the uncertainty, and used it as fuel to drive harder, to prove to themselves they could overcome. If you let self-doubt control your life, you're giving up before you even step onto the field. You're surrendering without a fight. In today's world, a lack of skill is a liability. The men who thrive are those who bring something unique, something valuable to the table. You can't afford to be a spectator. Skills are your currency, your leverage, and your edge. Whether it's financial literacy, physical fitness, emotional intelligence, or a trade, having skills gives you the confidence to navigate life's challenges, to stand firm in a world that's constantly changing. And when you bring this value to the table, people notice. Women notice. Employers notice. You gain respect not because of who you think you are, but because of what you can do. Financial Instability is The Fast Track to Disrespect in the modern market, as it demands more out of a man than ever before.

Money may not buy happiness, but financial instability will bring you nothing but hardship and insecurity. Being financially unstable isn't just about lacking funds; it's about lacking the discipline, the vision, and the ambition to build a secure life for yourself. The harsh truth is, if you don't have your finances in order, you're setting yourself up for a life of stress, dependency, and missed opportunities. Financial stability isn't about impressing anyone; it's about building a foundation that allows you to move through life with confidence, to invest in yourself, and to protect what you've worked hard to achieve.

The Impact of Inaction

Research shows that complacency leads to stagnation. A study published in the Journal of Personality and Social Psychology emphasizes that self-regulation and the pursuit of goals are essential for personal growth. Men who adopt a lazy mindset tend to avoid challenges, leading to skill deficits and reduced employability in an increasingly competitive job market. When it comes to dating, this translates to a lack of confidence and a diminished ability to engage meaningfully with women. Skill Deficiency can and will emerge overtime because of inaction and lack of effort. Remember A lack of skills not only limits career prospects but also affects a man's confidence in dating scenarios. Men with lower self-esteem often struggle to connect authentically with potential partners, perpetuating a cycle of loneliness and frustration. Financial stability is a significant factor in modern relationships, especially in a monetized dating environment. Research by the American Psychological Association highlights that financial stress can lead to anxiety and decreased life satisfaction. For men who are broke or financially unstable, this stress can manifest in various detrimental ways such as Reduced Attractiveness. Studies indicate that financial success often correlates with perceived desirability. When men lack financial stability, they are less likely to attract partners who are interested in long-term relationships, forcing them into a cycle of short-term transactions that further perpetuates their financial issues. You also run the risk of developing a Dependency on Quick Fixes, as Men who are financially unstable might resort to quick fixes for emotional satisfaction, such as casual encounters, which offer temporary pleasure but fail to provide long-term fulfillment. This behavior can lead to a vicious cycle of financial instability and emotional emptiness. The Advantage of Discipline is ultimately Skill Development and Financial Abundance the Power of Self-Discipline is not emphasized enough, or at least not until a man's back is against the wall in certain life situations. In stark contrast, men who prioritize skill development, physical fitness, emotional intelligence, and financial stability will find themselves with maximum leverage in today's dating landscape. Research consistently shows that self-discipline is a critical predictor of success. According to psychologist Angela Duckworth's work on grit, the ability to persevere and maintain focus on long-term goals is essential for achieving significant outcomes in life. Building Skills: Men who invest time in developing skills not only enhance their employability but also increase their confidence in various aspects of life, including dating.

The more competent a man feels in his professional and personal life, the more attractive he becomes to potential partners.

Emotional Intelligence and Relationship Success

- **Emotional intelligence (EI)** plays a crucial role in navigating modern relationships. A study published in the Journal of Applied Psychology indicates that individuals with high emotional intelligence tend to have better interpersonal skills, leading to more successful relationships. For men, this translates to:

- **Improved Communication:** Men who develop emotional intelligence can express their needs and desires more effectively, fostering deeper connections with partners. This ability to communicate creates an environment where meaningful relationships can thrive, as opposed to superficial transactional encounters.

- **Resilience in Relationships:** High emotional intelligence allows men to manage stress, navigate conflicts, and maintain emotional stability in challenging situations, making them more appealing partners. This resilience can help men avoid the pitfalls of toxic relationships that often ensnare those who lack emotional awareness.

Financial Abundance: The Key to Empowerment

Financial stability is not merely a personal achievement; it significantly influences a man's dating prospects. A report by the Pew Research Center indicates that both men and women perceive financial stability as an essential factor in romantic relationships.

- **Leverage and Choice:** Men who cultivate financial abundance have the leverage to choose partners wisely. They can invest in relationships that are meaningful rather than transactional, leading to healthier, more fulfilling connections. Moreover, financial abundance allows men to engage in enriching experiences that foster genuine connections, rather than relying on superficial transactions.

- **Avoiding Pitfalls of Instant Gratification:** Men who focus on building wealth and investing in their futures are less likely to be lured by the immediate gratification of casual encounters. They understand that true fulfillment comes from investing time and energy in their personal development and building lasting relationships.

The SUM: A Fork in the Road

The monetized dating era presents a stark choice for men: they can either succumb to complacency and risk losing everything, or they can embrace the challenge of self-improvement, skill acquisition, and financial stability to thrive in this new landscape. Lazy, self-doubting, unskilled, and financially unstable men will find themselves at a disadvantage, struggling to navigate a world that demands more than mere charm. In contrast, those who harness their discipline, cultivate emotional intelligence, and strive for financial abundance will emerge not just as players in the dating game but as the prize themselves. Ultimately, the choice is clear: invest in yourself and reap the rewards or continue down the path of complacency and watch as opportunities slip away. In the end, the man who is committed to personal growth and resilience will not only survive but thrive, navigating the complexities of modern relationships with confidence and purpose. The modern dating landscape, like life itself, has no sympathy for the complacent. It's designed to weed out the lazy, the unskilled, and the self-doubting. Men who are content to drift along, hoping something will change, are in for a harsh wake-up call. This isn't the time to make excuses or wait for the world to hand you something you haven't earned. This is the time to rise, to grind, and to build yourself into a man of substance.

09 |

THE POWER OF PENIS DISCIPLINE

Historical and Modern Accounts of Success Through Resisting Temptation

"Penis discipline," or the ability to control sexual urges and prioritize long-term goals over short-term gratification, has been a crucial element of success for many men throughout history. This concept embodies the idea that mastering one's sexual desires can lead to enhanced focus, improved decision-making, and greater overall success. Let's explore historical and modern examples that illustrate how this discipline has propelled men ahead of their peers. The discipline to control sexual urges—what we're calling "penis discipline"—isn't just about abstinence for its own sake. It's about harnessing the most primal, raw energy within you and turning it into fuel for a larger purpose. Men who've mastered this can channel that energy into focused ambition, achieving things that men enslaved by their desires can only dream of. This isn't new wisdom, either. History, spiritual teachings, and modern research have shown that a man's success often hinges on his ability to practice restraint and prioritize long-term gains over short-term pleasures. The concept of "brahmacharya" in ancient Eastern philosophy teaches that by preserving one's sexual energy, a man can reach higher states of mental clarity, spiritual power, and self-discipline. Traditionally, it emphasizes the redirection of sexual energy toward self-improvement, self-knowledge, and service. In a sense, it's a spiritual discipline that values channeling life force, or "vital energy," into constructive pursuits. Figures in various spiritual traditions, from Eastern sages to Western thinkers like Nikola Tesla, have shown us that reserving sexual energy fuels ambition, creativity, and resilience. Brahmacharya isn't about denying desire, but about mastering it. Clinical literature supports the positive psychological effects of this discipline, with findings indicating that redirecting sexual energy can enhance cognitive function, reduce stress, and heighten self-control. When sexual desire is harnessed rather than indulged at every whim, men report stronger focus and a sense of stability—mental qualities that are indispensable for achieving big goals. We can look at many modern figures who've attributed their success to this principle of sexual discipline. Athletes, executives, and artists have been vocal about the role of controlling impulses and prioritizing their work or mission over personal pleasures. The "no fap" movement, which encourages men to abstain from pornography and self-gratification, speaks to a modern recognition of the toll unchecked sexual indulgence can take on a man's drive, mental health, and resilience. Athletes like Muhammad Ali practiced sexual discipline, often abstaining for long stretches to maintain his mental and physical edge. In doing so, Ali harnessed a form of self-control that allowed him to withstand the rigors of his sport and stay at the top of his game. There's also documented evidence of improved focus and mental clarity for men who practice retention and direct that energy into their work. Studies on dopamine and reward pathways show that excessive sexual gratification can lead to desensitization and decreased motivation.

Men who abstain or limit these activities often report heightened alertness, more sustained focus, and a deeper sense of purpose.

Historical Accounts of Success Through Sexual Restraint

Socrates: A Philosopher of Restraint

Socrates, one of the foundational figures in Western philosophy, exemplified the power of self-control and discipline. Known for his commitment to wisdom over pleasure, Socrates often emphasized the importance of the mind over bodily desires. He believed that true happiness comes from virtue and knowledge, not from succumbing to physical temptations.

Impact on Success: Socrates' teachings laid the groundwork for critical thinking and self-examination, inspiring countless future philosophers, leaders, and thinkers. His ability to resist the allure of pleasure and focus on intellectual pursuits led to an enduring legacy, influencing Western thought for centuries.

Benjamin Franklin: A Founding Father with Focus

Benjamin Franklin, a polymath and one of the Founding Fathers of the United States, recognized the importance of self-discipline in achieving success. Franklin famously said, "Energy and persistence conquer all things." Throughout his life, he prioritized education, invention, and public service over fleeting pleasures.

Sexual Restraint: Franklin did engage in relationships, but he understood the value of balance and often refrained from excessive indulgence. His focus on self-improvement, financial literacy, and community engagement allowed him to make significant contributions to American society, from the founding of libraries to the development of the post office.

King Solomon: Wisdom Over Temptation

King Solomon, a biblical figure renowned for his wisdom, faced numerous temptations throughout his life, including romantic entanglements with many women. Despite his eventual downfall attributed to succumbing to temptation, his early reign showcased an exemplary approach to self-control.

Initial Success: Solomon's wisdom brought prosperity and peace to Israel, demonstrating how restraint in his early years allowed him to govern effectively and make profound contributions to society, including the construction of the First Temple. His story serves as a cautionary tale about the consequences of losing focus, highlighting the importance of maintaining discipline throughout one's life.

Modern-Day Examples of Discipline Leading to Success

Warren Buffett: The Investment Guru's Focus

Warren Buffett, one of the most successful investors of all time, attributes much of his success to self-discipline and focus. Known for his frugality and disciplined lifestyle, Buffett avoids impulsive decisions that often derail others in the financial realm.

Controlled Lifestyle: Buffett famously still lives in the same house he purchased decades ago and maintains a lifestyle that emphasizes savings and wise investments over lavish expenditures. His ability to resist the temptation of living extravagantly has allowed him to accumulate vast wealth and influence.

David Goggins: The Ultimate Accountability Mindset

David Goggins, a former Navy SEAL, ultramarathon runner, and motivational speaker, is renowned for his extreme discipline and focus on personal growth. Goggins emphasizes mental toughness and the importance of resisting comfort and temptation.

Mastering the Mind: Goggins has spoken about how mastering his urges, including sexual ones, has allowed him to push beyond perceived limits and achieve remarkable feats of endurance and achievement. His philosophy encourages others to prioritize long-term goals over immediate gratification.

Elon Musk: Innovation through Focus

Elon Musk, the CEO of Tesla and SpaceX, is known for his relentless work ethic and focus on innovation. Musk's success is attributed not only to his intelligence but also to his ability to stay disciplined in the pursuit of his goals, often at the expense of personal relationships and fleeting pleasures.

Prioritizing Vision: Musk's dedication to transforming industries—from electric vehicles to space exploration—demonstrates how the ability to prioritize long-term objectives over short-term indulgences can lead to extraordinary success. His work ethic and focus have positioned him as one of the most influential figures in modern technology.

Why Discipline Equals Freedom in a Man's Life

Discipline isn't about limiting yourself; it's about freeing yourself from control by external influences. When you allow your life to be dictated by immediate desires, you are at the mercy of those desires. But by practicing penis discipline, you become free to focus on what truly matters: your goals, your growth, and your legacy. Clinical literature on self-control shows that men with higher impulse control tend to be more successful across different areas of life—be it financially, socially, or personally. They're able to endure challenges because they aren't swayed by every whim or urge.

Practical Steps to Building Penis Discipline

- **Recognize Your Triggers:** Understanding what tempts you and why it is the first step toward controlling it. Identify situations or environments that lead to impulsive behavior and start rethinking how you approach them.

- **Redirect Your Energy:** When you feel the urge to indulge in sexual release or seek gratification, take that energy and pour it into something constructive. This could be hitting the gym, developing a skill, working on a business idea, or even practicing mindfulness. Redirecting urges into productive outlets builds the muscle of discipline while also giving you something tangible to show for your restraint.

- **Set Clear Goals:** Without a vision or set of goals, discipline can feel like a chore rather than a choice. Define what you want to achieve—whether it's financial success, physical health, or building a legacy. Make those goals vivid in your mind, so they become the reasons for maintaining your discipline. Having a purpose transforms self-control from restriction into empowerment.

- **Track Your Progress:** Keep a journal or set up a tracking system to see how consistent you are with retaining your focus and channeling your energy. Studies show that when we measure our progress, we're more likely to stick with it. This isn't just about keeping score but recognizing your growth and staying aware of the improvements in focus, mood, and motivation that follow disciplined behavior.

- **Practice Mindfulness and Meditation:** Mindfulness techniques, like meditation, teach you to observe your thoughts without being swept away by them. This builds a mental buffer that keeps you from reacting impulsively. Meditation can be particularly effective for cultivating self-discipline, as it strengthens the neural pathways that support restraint and decision-making.

In today's hyper-sexualized culture, distractions are everywhere, and the pull of instant gratification is strong. It takes a modern warrior to master his mind and his impulses. By exercising penis discipline, you're separating yourself from the pack. This clarity allows you to evaluate situations and relationships from a position of power and self-control rather than being a slave to urges.

Think about it: men who chase every fleeting pleasure—whether it's from women, pornography, or casual hookups—are constantly draining their energy and clouding their judgment. They're at the mercy of impulse, forever caught in a cycle of instant reward and long-term regret. But a man who learns to control his desires gains a vantage point few others ever reach. This self-mastery turns you into a focused, resilient individual, ready to face any challenge. History is filled with examples of men who practiced sexual discipline as a way to achieve greatness. Whether it was the warrior monks who dedicated themselves to martial arts, inventors like Nikola Tesla who channeled their energy into innovation, or philosophers who chose celibacy to deepen their concentration, these men understood the power that comes from mastery over self. Their lives teach us that real power doesn't come from indulging in every desire, but in having the discipline to choose the path less traveled. Today, that choice means resisting the distractions of instant gratification in all its forms and focusing on building something that lasts.

The Psychological Underpinning of Penis Discipline

Research in psychology supports the notion that self-control and discipline can significantly influence success. A study published in Psychological Science found that individuals with high self-control tend to achieve better outcomes in various life domains, including academics, health, and relationships. Delayed Gratification is practical manifestation magic. The famous Marshmallow Test conducted by psychologist Walter Mischel illustrates the power of delayed gratification. Children who were able to resist the immediate temptation of a marshmallow for the promise of two later demonstrated greater success in adulthood, showcasing the long-term benefits of self-discipline.

The SUM: The Value of Resisting Temptation

The historical and modern examples of men who have practiced penis discipline illustrate that mastering one's sexual urges can lead to profound success. From philosophers and political leaders to contemporary innovators and athletes, the ability to prioritize long-term goals over immediate gratification is a common thread among those who have achieved greatness. In the current era, where instant gratification and superficial relationships abound, men who cultivate discipline, focus, and resilience stand to gain a significant advantage. By embracing the power of penis discipline, they can harness their energy toward achieving their ambitions, ultimately positioning themselves as leaders in their respective fields and in the dating landscape.

The Spare Change

If you're out here in the dating marketplace, understand that it's not just about getting lost in a pretty face or getting sidetracked by what she's flaunting. Real talk: if you're going to dive into this game, you better have a strategy that includes self-preservation. That means establishing principles for your own protection, and one critical move that most men overlook is "aftercare." Yeah, I know, some of you might think that's strictly BDSM stuff, but hear me out. This is about safeguarding your peace of mind and creating a dynamic that keeps your energy protected. In today's dating market—especially when dealing with women accustomed to the "monetized" scene—aftercare isn't just a nice-to-have; it's essential.

So, what is Aftercare?

Aftercare is that period after any intimate experience where you, as the man, take a moment to center yourself and check in with both parties involved. It's not just about a post-encounter chat or cuddling; it's about establishing closure and clarity on both ends. Think of it like a cooldown after a workout—you need it to prevent strain or injury, both physically and mentally. In the context of the monetized dating scene, aftercare isn't only for her benefit. It's a practice that keeps you clear-headed, avoiding miscommunication or unnecessary drama. This is about looking out for your energy, creating boundaries, and ensuring mutual respect in what can often be a transactional setup. If you're dealing with "monetized" women—women who have clear expectations of exchange, whether it's time, money, or some form of tangible benefit—you're already in a different realm of dating. This market has its own set of unspoken rules, and one misstep can lead to assumptions or resentment. Aftercare is your tool for preventing any misinterpretation. By setting aside time to acknowledge what just went down, you're drawing a clear line between casual encounters and anything more profound. You're stating, "This was an experience, not a promise." And for those of you serious about your time and energy, this is how you avoid unnecessary entanglements. From a psychological standpoint, aftercare helps ground both parties and allows them to process their feelings and expectations clearly. For men, aftercare can be a moment of reflection—a way to understand any emotional after-effects before jumping back into the grind. You're taking control of the narrative and avoiding any afterthoughts that might cloud your focus. Women, too, benefit from aftercare because it signals respect, regardless of whether the exchange was casual or not. It keeps resentment, disappointment, or confusion out of the picture because you've taken the time to acknowledge the experience without any ambiguity. For you as a man, aftercare is about self-protection. It's a chance to reinforce your boundaries and recalibrate mentally. When you skip this step, you risk carrying extra emotional weight that you don't need, especially in a market that's all about calculated exchanges. Aftercare helps you avoid anger, resentment, or confusion, allowing you to keep your mind clear and your focus intact. In a time when distractions are everywhere and energy is currency, protecting your peace should be non-negotiable. If you're out here navigating the modern dating market, understand that aftercare is a tool for your benefit. It's about staying intentional with your time, your energy, and your boundaries. Establishing this practice is about safeguarding your emotional currency, sidestepping unnecessary misunderstandings, and making sure that whatever you're involved in is kept in perspective. Remember: the dating marketplace might be monetized, but your peace and focus are priceless. rough variety (choking, scratching, biting, slapping, spitting, finger usage etc... In the moment when the adrenaline is flowing your both happily engaged with one another. However, females can be fickle creatures that have a hard time coming down and making a simple disconnect from physical activities such as sex

10 |

SURROGACY
The New age Legacy Opportunity for Men?

This might come as a surprise to many guys reading this but, Surrogacy has emerged as a viable option for individuals and couples seeking to have children when traditional means are not possible or desirable. This path to parenthood has gained traction, especially among men who wish to leave a legacy but face challenges in establishing viable marriage options in the Western Hemisphere due to the monetization of relationships. This topic might seem very taboo, especially for younger males that aren't done getting thrashed by the marketplace yet, to say the least, however it has slowly started to emerge as a viable option for those men seeking legacy without the dangers of dealing with the bias family court mafia found here in the west. This option while non-traditional, by nature grants a man a direct line to succession without having to hear the dreaded "you should've chosen better" after the woman whom you decided to love and care for wakes up and decides to cash in her leverage via your child. For example: When it comes to passing down wealth without the hassle, a **"Revocable Trust"** is a powerful tool, especially for the man who's calculated, strategic, and serious about building a legacy. We're talking about setting up the kind of generational wealth that sidesteps the probate circus and eliminates the potential for legal entanglements with a surrogate mother or anyone else trying to step in. This is about securing what's yours and ensuring that your child receives it in the cleanest, most efficient way possible.

What is a Revocable Trust, and Why Should You Care?

A revocable trust is a legal entity that holds your assets while you're alive, allowing you to manage them on your terms and change or "revoke" it if needed. Think of it as an iron-clad vessel that protects your wealth, real estate, investments, or any other assets you want to safeguard. When you're gone, these assets seamlessly transfer to your child without the mess of probate or outside interference. Research from The Journal of Financial Service Professionals backs this up: people who establish trusts cut probate costs and waiting times by over 90%. A well-structured revocable trust is the definition of "having your cake and eating it too" — you maintain full control now, while guaranteeing your child's future without unnecessary delays or expenses. Some will read this and still say; Why This Trust is Ideal for Surrogate-Born Children?

Since the child is born through a surrogate, this setup becomes even more valuable. There's no chance for the surrogate mother to interfere with the trust or make any claims over assets. In legal terms, a revocable trust sidesteps traditional inheritance disputes because, unlike a will, it's difficult for anyone to contest. You're effectively creating a direct line from your hard-earned assets to your child. Studies show that traditional probate can take up to 16 months to complete, but a revocable trust transfers assets almost instantly upon death. That's a direct advantage to your child, who won't have to wade through the delays and costs that typically plague inheritance cases. For a man who's sacrificed and built something real, this approach ensures the wealth goes where it's intended—uncontested, immediate, and hassle-free.

How to Set Up a Revocable Trust

(Steps to Cement Your Legacy)

Setting up trust doesn't have to be a legal headache. Here's how you do it in a way that maximizes benefit for your child:

- **Choose a Trustee:** Select someone responsible to manage the trust if you're unable to do so. Many people opt for a trusted family member or financial advisor, but some go with a bank or financial institution for added protection.

- **Fund the Trust:** Transfer your assets into the trust—property, investments, cash. By funding trust now, you're taking assets out of your personal estate, effectively shielding them from potential inheritance taxes or probate.

- **Outline Distribution Terms:** Lay out specifics. This is where you establish how and when assets are given to your child. You might decide on lump sums or incremental payments at certain life milestones. Case studies show that structured distribution often leads to more financially stable offspring, as they receive resources responsibly rather than all at once.

- **Designate a Guardian if Necessary:** Since your child is surrogate born, it's wise to specify a guardian who will act in their best interests if they're still a minor at the time of your passing.

Legal experts consistently confirm that revocable trusts allow for smoother and faster asset transitions, significantly reducing financial risk for heirs and eliminating the typical familial conflicts that come with probate. We're not in the business of playing it small anymore as men...the time has come to get educated and play like a big dog.

Real-World Examples

"Building a Bulletproof Legacy"

The Rockefeller family is a prime example of how trusts effectively build and pass down generational wealth. Their use of trusts—primarily revocable ones—helped ensure the family's vast fortunes were handed down through generations with minimal taxes or disputes. Studies have found that families utilizing trust structures preserve an average of 20-30% more wealth across generations than those using traditional wills. This is the level of smart asset protection you're aiming for. Another example is the case of Robert F. Smith, billionaire philanthropist, who reportedly uses similar trust structures to manage his family's assets. By leveraging revocable trusts, he guarantees that his wealth is directed where he wants, regardless of outside pressures or potential legal disputes.

How Your Child Directly Benefits from This Setup

By setting up a revocable trust, you're clearing a path for your child that's free from the usual red tape. This is bigger than just protecting assets; it's about giving your child a head start, free from the costs, delays, and potential risks associated with probate. Another perk to this investment vehicle is Immediate Access, meaning the assets are instantly available to the beneficiary, cutting out the probate process and its associated costs, which, according to the American Bar Association, can eat up to 5% of the estate's value. Revokable trust also has the benefit of Reduced Taxes long with bypassing some estate taxes, potentially saving significant amounts, which means your child inherits more of what you intended for them. The trust also offers Guaranteed Privacy which is another major benefit to consider as Probate is public record; meaning anyone can see who inherited what. Trust, however, is private. This shields your child's inheritance from public view, protecting them from unwanted attention or exploitation. You'd essentially be giving the child a direct line with everything you worked hard to build for their benefit.

Setting up a revocable trust gives you control now, ensures your wealth is preserved, and directly benefits your child without them having to fight through bureaucracy or familial disputes. For a man focused on building real, sustainable value, this is how you preserve the empire you worked so hard to create. You don't leave it to chance; you build the foundation for generations to come—efficiently, privately, and strategically. By examining the costs of

ANTHONY R BARBER JR.

surrogacy in different countries, particularly the Philippines and the USA, we can better understand how this option can provide a streamlined pathway for men interested in building a family legacy.

Cost Breakdown:
Surrogacy in the Philippines vs. USA

Surrogacy in the Philippines

Surrogacy in the Philippines is a growing industry, and the cost is significantly lower than in the United States. Here's a breakdown of the typical expenses:

- **Total Cost:** The total cost of surrogacy in the Philippines ranges from $30,000 to $50,000. This package often includes medical expenses, legal fees, and compensation for the surrogate.

- **Surrogate Compensation:** Surrogates in the Philippines are typically compensated between $10,000 and $15,000. This compensation is often seen to support the surrogate's family while enabling them to participate in the surrogacy process.

- **Legal Fees:** Legal fees for surrogacy contracts and the establishment of parental rights can range from $5,000 to $10,000.

- **Medical Expenses:** Medical costs, including in vitro fertilization (IVF) and prenatal care, typically add another $15,000 to $25,000 to the total. The availability of quality healthcare at a lower cost makes the Philippines an attractive option for prospective parents.

Surrogacy in the USA

In contrast, surrogacy in the United States is significantly more expensive:

- **Total Cost:** The total cost of surrogacy in the USA typically ranges from $100,000 to $200,000. This stark difference can be attributed to higher medical expenses, legal fees, and surrogate compensation.

- **Surrogate Compensation:** Surrogates in the USA are compensated between $30,000 and $50,000 on average. This figure can increase based on the surrogate's experience, health, and specific agreement.

- **Legal Fees:** Legal fees can reach upwards of $20,000, given the complexity of contracts and the need for thorough legal representation to ensure parental rights are established.

- **Medical Expenses:** Medical expenses in the USA can exceed $50,000, primarily due to high healthcare costs and insurance premiums.

The Streamlined Option for Men Seeking Legacy

With the growing cost disparity between surrogacy options in the Philippines and the USA, men interested in building a legacy may find surrogacy in the Philippines to be a more appealing solution. Here's how it can serve as an effective option:

Access to Parenthood Without Traditional Marriage

In today's monetized dating landscape, many men struggle to find suitable partners for long-term relationships or marriage. The complexity of modern dating, marked by superficial interactions and transactional relationships, can leave men without a clear path to parenthood. Surrogacy provides a way for these men to bypass traditional obstacles and take proactive steps toward fatherhood. This unorthodox method provides an avenue for a man to maintain a Controlled Environment, allowing men to have greater control over the process of becoming a parent. They can choose a surrogate based on health, compatibility, and mutual understanding, ensuring that they are involved in the creation of their family.

Legacy Building and Mentorship Opportunities

The opportunity to have biological children through surrogacy opens the door for men to leave a legacy. By investing in surrogacy, men can create a family they can mentor, guide, and pass down their values, knowledge, and resources to. You as a father can Streamline Financial Preparation for Offspring without outside interference, gaslighting from the financial illiterate and unprepared types: By saving costs through surrogacy in the Philippines for example, men can allocate funds for their child's education, inheritance, and personal development. This forward-thinking approach allows them to provide a stable and enriching environment for their future heirs. There's also a Long-Term Impact to utilizing this method. Men who focus on creating a family through surrogacy can establish a strong legacy, fostering personal growth and character development in their children. They can mentor them in their professional and personal lives, ensuring the continuation of their values and aspirations. Many feminists, and the system itself will read this chapter and feel directly threatened and that's the point my "G". No point in pulling punches with this new emerging landscape. Men need all the roadmaps and options they can get their hands on.

The Streamlined Processes

As the demand for surrogacy increases, particularly in countries like the Philippines, the industry is likely to become more streamlined and efficient. Innovations in medical technology, improved legal frameworks, and the establishment of reputable agencies can further enhance the surrogacy experience. Make no mistake about it as this is indeed an Emerging Market: As more men and couples turn to surrogacy, the industry is expected to grow, leading to more competitive pricing and better services. This trend could result in a more accessible option for those seeking to become parents without the traditional barriers posed by marriage. Surprisingly you're seeing more Cultural Acceptance, as far as men being open to the option: The growing acceptance of diverse family structures and parenting methods will likely foster a supportive environment for surrogacy moving forward, making it a viable option for men seeking to leave a legacy without the constraints of traditional relationships.

The SUM: A New Path to Legacy

The stark contrast in surrogacy costs between the Philippines and the USA presents an opportunity for men interested in creating a legacy. By investing in surrogacy, men can bypass the challenges of modern dating, secure their desire for fatherhood, and ultimately contribute positively to their offspring's lives. Surrogacy allows for the construction of a family unit where mentorship, guidance, and inheritance can thrive, offering a path to legacy that aligns with contemporary realities. In a world where viable marriage options may be diminishing, surrogacy represents a forward-thinking approach to building a meaningful life and future. As this option continues to evolve, men will find that they can forge their paths toward parenthood and legacy with confidence and purpose. Again, this is just an example of a pivot point/option you as a man have when and if you decide to leave your legacy to an offspring. This is not any attempt to condemn females or the power of traditional mating, but rather expanding the viewpoints and perspectives a man has at their disposal when the market fails to satisfy normal avenues of procreation.

11 |

ALL MEN PAY
Pseudo Romance vs. Leading with Leverage

Let's be real about something most men are too afraid to admit: All men pay. It doesn't matter what corner of life you stand on—you pay to play. The debate rages on about how the so-called "Pookie, "Ray-Ray", Chad and Tyrone" types—those broke, aimless dudes—seem to get sex for free while hard-working men are left out in the cold, digging into their wallets or their emotional reserves to get even a sliver of attention. But let me break it down for you—there's no free lunch in the world of women. These "free riders" pay too. Some men caught up in the Red Pill rhetoric might say, "Women prefer giving it up to these low-status dudes without real leverage." They'll argue that the women are giving intimacy to these men while holding out on the resourceful men who've built something for themselves. But let's zoom out for a second women have always been in survival mode, and survival is the ultimate game of leverage. When you're broke, purposeless, or a man of no real ambition, it's easy to think some dudes get off without paying. But trust me—they're paying too, in ways that are far more costly than money. Once a man gets focused on those things which matter most...the clever feminine acting becomes repulsive the man of worth. At some point her Survival Game cover is blown, the theater Mask Comes Off. After all, the mask must come off at some point, because even they can't fake it for that long. As time moves on and the biological clock ticks, women often change the game to hunt once their sexual marketplace value decreases below a certain point.

Don't twist or misconstrue this fact with total loss, as even the most demonic females with a checked past and present can pack up their emotional hang-ups long enough to manipulate a desperate, lonely gump/simp type into falling for them (they always have a safety net). When they're younger and have time on their side, they can afford to be selective. They'll choose the bad boy, the wild card, the one who isn't giving much back but gives them that spark of excitement because his life mirrors her life via drama, violence, struggle, strife etc... But as the years pass, that neck-snapping, loud-mouth bravado? It's suddenly replaced with a mask of humility—a false front of being cooperative, "independent," and ready for commitment. Why? Because she's watching the wall approach. That wall represents her fading leverage. And as her friends settle down and build families, she sees herself being left behind, scrambling for options. This is why women change their approach—they realize they need to find the man they once disregarded as lame, the man they once had no time for. This man, who's been building himself up in silence, suddenly becomes the most desirable option, but as a man you shouldn't worry about being desired, chosen, or picked, because all those things are a side effect of leverage.

Make no mistake, as in her eyes you are still viewed as lame to her, your attractiveness when up for genetic survival reasons based on your resources and accomplishments in life. If you never given them anything to talk about that create separation between you and other men, you're hustling backwards. While men generally pursue sex for pleasure, women approach sex as a tool of leverage. The feminine Power Play: (Intimacy as Leverage) is about control, manipulation, and even long-term exploitation. Women know that sex is their greatest weapon in the game of power, after all we otherwise avoid them if not for the pursuit of sex, and or reproduction. They use (Intimacy as Leverage) not just for physical satisfaction but to place men in positions of vulnerability. Men have all the leverage over women until two things take place, with one of those things being pregnancy, and the second being marriage. Let's not sugarcoat it—the risk of STDs/STIs, the possibility of pregnancy, and the fear of being tied to the wrong woman for life are very real for men, especially in the western hemisphere. Pregnancy, for example, is an investment for women. They will gladly subject themselves to nine months of discomfort, all with the goal of leveraging that child as a lifelong anchor, turning men into resource-providers without the woman ever truly reciprocating on an emotional or supportive level, effectively transforming a loving husband into a wage slave monitored by the police state for 18 years minimum. According to research from the American Sociological Review, this is often described as the "breadwinner's burden," where men are locked into the role of provider, while the woman's contribution diminishes once the man is trapped into long-term financial and emotional commitments.

Psychological manipulation becomes a subtle, ongoing process where a man's resources are drained over time, and he is met with non-stop passive-aggressiveness by his abuser until a crash out moment happens or Divorce. The Financial Trap is usually seen very early by men within toxic and unfulfilling relationships but due to a man's inherently loving and protective nature we endure relationship hardships for the sake for legacy and stability. In many ways, men allow themselves to be played. We chase women, even though we hold the ultimate prize—our resources, our discipline, our ability to create and sustain wealth and security. Women might be able to out-earn men in specific circumstances, but without the guidance of a resourceful, disciplined man, their financial futures are often shaky. Studies from the Journal of Financial Planning show that women, despite increasing their earning power, still face significant challenges in long-term financial planning, often due to impulsive spending habits or a lack of mentorship in saving and investing. We, as men, hold the key to sustainable outcomes, and yet, we are so often fooled by the illusion of love, trapped by sex, and manipulated into providing for women who've done nothing but show us disrespect during their prime years.

Let's talk about The Power of Leverage, because that's the only way a man survives and thrives in this new landscape. Men of value, men with resources and discipline, don't have to bow down to these traps. Men with penis discipline—those who can resist the lure of easy sex, who can see through the superficial charm and seduction—are the ones who come out on top. Look at historical figures like Alexander the Great and Julius Caesar—both had their moments of temptation but ultimately rose above it. Caesar resisted the wiles of Cleopatra long enough to build an empire, while other men fell under her spell and were ruined. In the modern world, men like LeBron James and David Beckham have exhibited similar discipline. They built their legacies through focus, ignoring the distractions of fleeting pleasure. While their peers fell into scandals and broke under the weight of their impulses, these men doubled down on their purpose and built lasting wealth, influence, and legacy. Leverage is King At the end of the day, and all men must pay the cost for such things (time, energy, attention, and money). But the real question is: what are you paying for? Are you paying with your time, your energy, your money, and your peace of mind to a woman? Or are you making strategic investments that give you control and leverage in the future? Women are masters of survival, but if a man can rise above the superficial, develop his purpose, and master his desires, he becomes untouchable as far as the opposite sex is concerned. That type of man is secure in himself, not just his masculinity, he is secure in thought and action, which ranks him miles above the average male. This monetized dating landscape isn't the death of the modern man—it's the awakening. Women's true motives are no longer hidden, and that's a good thing. Now you can see the game for what it is. We no longer must pretend, chase, or submit to a world that wants men to pay with everything you've worked for, with little to zero return on the back end or front-end. Instead, modern males can sample the goods—pay for an hour of pleasure and move on, no strings attached. Many conditioned males of today, and yesteryear will claim this is "Tricking" or "Simping" (newly adopted buzzwords of the day), but if it saves you peace of mind, and a boatload of resources overall this is a good way to incrementally experience female energy in its raw form. You get to focus on building your empire, developing your skillset, and pursuing your life purpose. When you do that, when you rise above the games and distractions, you become the real prize. Trust me, when you stand in your power and purpose, the same women who once ignored you will now be the ones chasing, but by then, you'll have something far more valuable than their approval—you'll have leverage. The modern dating landscape, especially with the rise of the monetized sexual marketplace, has forced men to confront harsh realities about female motivations. Many men are now opting for a more direct approach, bypassing the pseudo-romance narrative that's been passed down through generations. While it might seem unconventional, the logic behind it is undeniable as men are realizing, often painfully, that "the woman doesn't really want me, but she does want my resources.

In this hyper-sexualized culture, many men are coming to terms with the fact that transactional exchanges—where resources are swapped for time, attention, or physical intimacy—are no longer hidden beneath the veneer of romance. The question, "How much for your time?", may well become standard in the future as men pivot from emotional investments to direct exchanges with better ROI (return on investment) in both the short and long term.

Psychological Feasibility of Direct Transactions

From a psychological perspective, men who adopt this approach are tapping into a biological cost-benefit analysis ingrained in human behavior. According to evolutionary psychology, men historically competed for access to mates through displays of resources, strength, and capability. In modern times, these displays manifest as wealth, status, and power. Women, in turn, assess these traits as markers of a man's ability to provide stability and security. However, when this dynamic is laid bare, as it is in today's monetized market, men begin to cut through the emotional pretense. Behavioral economics supports this shift, as men begin to look at relationships through the lens of utility maximization—what gives them the best return with the least investment? Many men, already disillusioned by costly, resource-draining relationships, find that direct exchanges present a more rational, predictable, and efficient path toward satisfying their biological desires. Studies from the Kinsey Institute and the Journal of Sex Research show that men often engage in short-term mating strategies when they perceive that long-term investments will not pay off. In a culture that is increasingly monetized and hyper-sexualized, this shift toward direct transactions becomes not just feasible but attractive. Men can achieve their goals—whether for physical pleasure, companionship, or novelty—without the long-term financial and emotional drains that accompany traditional relationships.

Why The "Transactional" Model Will Likely Dominate in the Future

1. Economic Efficiency

As dating becomes more monetized, the emotional and financial costs of maintaining traditional relationships become glaring. The ROI for men in many long-term relationships is poor, with studies showing that men are increasingly unsatisfied with the imbalance of emotional labor and financial commitment required in modern partnerships. Direct transactions, in contrast, offer a clear-cut, no-strings-attached exchange where men maintain control over their resources while getting exactly what they're after without the emotional baggage.

2. Transparency and Honesty

One of the key arguments in favor of this shift is honesty. Many men are fed up with the deception inherent in the pseudo-romance game, where they are expected to "woo" women who ultimately seek financial security rather than genuine connection. The monetized dating market is laying bare the transactional nature of relationships, forcing both men and women to acknowledge the reality: resources are exchanged for access. Men increasingly prefer the direct approach because it removes the need for deception, manipulation, or posturing, creating a transactional clarity that is refreshingly honest.

3. Psychological Safety

There's also an argument to be made for psychological safety in this model. Men who have experienced relationship trauma, betrayal, or manipulation are less inclined to re-enter the traditional dating pool, where emotional vulnerability is required. Studies in the Journal of Personality and Social Psychology suggest that men who have been "burned" in past relationships often opt for low-risk, high-reward engagements in the future. A transactional approach to dating allows men to protect their mental and emotional well-being while still satisfying their physical needs.

4. Cultural Shift

The culture itself is shifting to reflect this new reality. With the rise of platforms like OnlyFans, Tinder, and Sugar Daddy arrangements, we are seeing a growing normalization of direct transactional relationships. These platforms explicitly market sex and companionship in exchange for money or gifts, removing the need for emotional attachment. As this model becomes more widespread and accepted, men will increasingly view direct exchanges as not just an option but a preferred strategy in the dating market.

The Future of the Monetized Dating Market

As this shift continues, the question "How much for your time?" will likely become standard for many men. They will see the long-term benefits of this approach, especially when compared to traditional dating, which often involves high upfront costs with little guarantee of a positive outcome. The direct transaction model offers immediate, predictable results, aligning with a man's goal of resource conservation and efficient use of his time. In fact, according to the Journal of Economic Behavior and Organization, men are already showing an increased willingness to spend money on short-term sexual gratification rather than investing in long-term relationships. The psychological toll of modern relationships, combined with the financial risk, means that men are naturally gravitating toward this more transactional approach.

Men have long been conditioned to view sex as something that must be "earned" through emotional labor and resource investment. But in the new reality, men are reclaiming their power by recognizing that the exchange of resources for time or intimacy is not "tricking"—it's simply economics. The sooner both men and women accept the realities of this marketplace, the clearer the path becomes for men to achieve their goals without being exploited emotionally or financially. At the end of the day, men who understand this shift will fare better in the long run. Traditional dating is no longer the most efficient use of time or resources in a world where intimacy and relationships are increasingly monetized. By cutting through the pseudo-romance, men can engage on their terms, setting boundaries and prioritizing their own growth and fulfillment. The return on investment—both emotionally and financially—will be much higher for those who adopt this approach, allowing them to remain focused on their purpose while still satisfying their needs via ROI of Direct Transactions. As this becomes more widespread, the direct transactional approach will become the new norm, a reflection of the evolving nature of relationships in the monetized sexual marketplace. Like the title states: All men pay. That's the truth of the modern dating landscape, and whether it's direct or indirect, the cost is real. Now let me break it down for you. Ask yourself, have you ever taken someone on a date? If the answer is yes, then chances are, you reached into your pocket. Right off the bat, you paid for that meal, the drinks, the entertainment— maybe all of the above. That's the first and most obvious form of payment:

financial. We're not done, as it doesn't stop there, not by a long shot. Think about what it took just to make that date happen. You had to initiate, right? You probably spent time setting the date and location, talking to her in the days or hours leading up to it. At that time, you could have invested in yourself, building your skills, working on your goals, stacking up your money. But instead, you carved out a piece of that precious time to line up for this opportunity. Payment, in the form of your time. Then there's the travel. You're driving to the spot, using fuel, wearing down your vehicle—yet again, this is money out of your pocket. Payment, once again, financially. Let's not forget the biggest expenditure of all: energy and attention. For you Casanovas and creative date planners out there, it's a whole other level. You're brainstorming ideas, putting thought and effort into crafting an experience she'll remember. You're trying to be that guy who stands out, but that takes real creative energy—mental capital you could've invested elsewhere, in the gym, in a side hustle, or in planning your next big move. That's payment in focus and creativity, and trust me, those are assets as valuable as money. Here's the kicker: these indirect costs often go unnoticed. Most men are so locked into the hunt, so deep into the pursuit, that they don't stop to see how fast these resources are slipping through their fingers. You're paying out time, energy, attention, and money on a date-to-date basis, yet many overlook this because they're busy chasing that fleeting validation, that temporary companionship. Now, I'm not saying don't date or don't enjoy life. But if you don't approach it with awareness, you're playing without leverage. Because making no mistake—every encounter, every interaction, costs you something.

The real question is: are you paying with leverage, or are you letting yourself get drained in exchange for a pseudo-romantic experience that might not serve you in the long run? Remember this: paying with awareness puts you in control. Paying without awareness leaves you vulnerable. Lead with leverage and ensure every choice you make aligns with your bigger purpose. That's how you level up. That's how you win. All men pay, but when it comes to husbands, the stakes get even higher. In marriage, the game changes, and the cost of investment goes far beyond what single men experience. Husbands ultimately pay the most, and not just financially—they pay with nearly every aspect of their lives. Once a man steps into marriage, he's no longer just funding a few dates; he's taking on a lifelong financial commitment. You're now responsible for the household expenses, and even if you're in a two-income situation, most husbands carry the weight of being the primary provider. Mortgage, bills, unexpected expenses, all these become constant in your financial outflow. And if the marriage breaks down? Divorce courts are often structured in a way that sees men parting with not only their assets but also a chunk of their future earnings through alimony and child support. The financial toll is relentless, and it's no longer indirect; it's right there in the open, month after month. The cost for husbands goes even deeper than money. Time and energy are another heavy investment. You're devoting yourself to building a life together, a home, possibly raising kids, and it's a 24/7 role. Many men find their time swallowed by responsibilities— maintaining the house, supporting their spouse emotionally, raising children. The dreams you once had, the time you used to have for yourself, even your hobbies and friendships, they start to fade into the background. Now, everything you do is woven into the fabric of this partnership, and often that comes with the sacrifice of personal ambition and freedom. Let's not overlook attention and focus, either. In a marriage, your energy isn't just yours to direct and utilize; it's always shared (). A husband often finds himself in the role of the problem solver, the emotional anchor, the steady foundation. But this requires continuous emotional investment, the kind of focus and mental bandwidth that, over the years, can drain a man if he's not careful. In a marriage, your attention isn't only directed at yourself or your growth; it's shared with your spouse's needs, her dreams, her goals. The path isn't just your own anymore, and that split focus can be costly if it comes at the expense of your personal development. Let's be real: most men are so focused on providing, supporting, and sustaining the relationship that they lose sight of the leverage they once held. They pay with autonomy and sometimes even their sense of self. Marriage isn't inherently negative, but a man who steps into it without understanding these costs can find himself paying in ways he never expected, especially if the relationship becomes strained. So, what's the takeaway? Husbands ultimately pay the highest price because marriage requires a lifelong commitment to time, energy, attention, and financial resources. But when you approach marriage with leverage, awareness, and a solid sense of who you are, you avoid the hidden costs. Marriage should elevate you, not drain you. And if you're mindful of what you're paying into, you're less likely to find yourself depleted. Lead with leverage, know your value, and make sure the cost of commitment aligns with your purpose.

12 |

MEN COMMIT / WOMEN SUBMIT
Dating Duality: Conditional vs. Absolute

In a world where the dating game's rules have changed drastically, this chapter dives into a concept that goes back to the foundations of human nature itself. For men, commitment is an investment—it's absolute, driven by loyalty, purpose, and an expectation of legacy. For women, however, submission is often conditional, dependent on factors like security, value, and the promise of stability. As men, we're wired to commit when we find something or someone worthy, but for women, that commitment hinges on circumstances that meet their needs. Studies in evolutionary psychology, like those published by David M. Buss and Cindy M. Meston, show that men and women approach relationships with deeply rooted, biologically driven motivations. Men seek to invest in partnerships that further their legacy or align with their purpose; when a man commits, it's because he sees potential in a future outcome—a future built on his terms. For women, studies show that submission is often motivated by a sense of safety and security, tied closely to what she "perceives" the man can provide, again adding to the perception is reality argument. While men pursue relationships looking to build and protect, women evaluate the potential in terms of what it offers them at that specific moment, which can range from petty pleasure seeking in their younger years to survival as they mature. Historically, This Duality Played Out on the Grandest of Scales. Take the example of Cleopatra and Julius Caesar which I touched on earlier. Here was a woman who submitted to Caesar's power because it secured her kingdom (Survival narrative). She leveraged her position as queen, yes, but it was conditional based on Caesar's political power and resources. Once that shifted, so did her submission. Caesar, on the other hand, was absolutely committed to his vision of Rome's expansion, investing himself fully in a mission that extended beyond personal gain (selfless Ambition), even as he ultimately misjudged how conditional her loyalty could be. In the Modern World, We See These Patterns Reinforced. Look at high-profile figures like Jeff Bezos. A man driven by his commitment to vision and legacy, Bezos devoted years to building Amazon. His investment in the company wasn't conditional—it was his life's purpose. Meanwhile, his relationship with Mackenzie Bezos eventually crumbled; she committed based on their alignment at one point in time, but as conditions changed, so did the nature of that commitment. And we see this play out in countless cases where a woman's submission depends on how well her partner's value meets her current needs. This isn't about one side being better or worse, it's about understanding that, in the dating marketplace (Historically or Modern era), men are the ones who must stay solid on their purpose, while women are often evaluating—adapting based on conditional needs.

Men must remain the Island, while women often play the waves violently crashing against the shoreline without fail. Science Backs up What we see play out every day. Research from the Journal of Marriage and Family indicates that men invest more heavily, both emotionally and financially, in long-term partnerships than women. Studies on conditional mating strategies, highlighted in Evolution and Human Behavior, support this; they show that women's attraction often fluctuates based on situational factors such as career stability, physical security, or social status. Men, meanwhile, tend to remain consistent in their drive to build and sustain relationships if they align with their purpose.

Why This Matters

For men navigating this modern dating landscape, recognizing the conditional nature of a woman's investment allows you to remain in control of your resources, energy, and most importantly, your purpose. Understanding this duality—where men commit absolutely, and women often submit conditionally—is a game changer. By acknowledging this fundamental difference, you become a strategist, not a victim of circumstances. In this chapter, we're breaking down this duality, bringing in the science, and using powerful examples, both historical and modern, to show why men who know their worth stay focused and stay winning, especially in the long run. When you move with purpose, you'll naturally recognize conditional versus absolute commitment, and that will shape how you choose to invest into your life, your energy, and your legacy. This isn't just about dating—it's about leverage, strategy, and the blueprint for a life that's unshakable. When a man decides to commit, it's absolute. This isn't a halfway move. A man's commitment means he's ready to put his time, resources, and loyalty on the line. He's building a legacy, staking his reputation, and in some cases, even risking his future. Men are wired this way—once they decide to be all-in, there's no second-guessing. He's dedicated to seeing it through, protecting what he values, and investing fully, with no strings attached. That's the essence of a man's commitment, it's driven by purpose and legacy, not conditions or convenience. Now, look at the flip side. A woman's submission, as much as we'd like to believe, it's the same as a man's commitment, often operates in a different lane. Submission, for many women, has a conditional, transactional layer to it. This doesn't necessarily mean it's about money in a direct sense, but the exchange runs deep. It could be access to security, status, or even the social position a man offers. She aligns herself with a man based on what he can bring to the table right now; that's why her loyalty, her effort, her energy can shift as quickly as the circumstances that attracted her in the first place.

Transactional by Nature, Not Just "Money on the Dresser."

Women are natural evaluators. Evolution and psychology back this up—women are biologically designed to prioritize security and value. When she's deciding whether to submit, it's not simply an emotional choice; it's a calculated assessment of resources, stability, and protection. Even when it's not direct "money on the dresser," she's sizing up the investment you're making, consciously or unconsciously considering what she's receiving in return. Her submission is often predicated on a series of trade-offs and exchanges that aren't the same for men. Where men invest with a long-term, unconditional vision, women's investment tends to ebb and flow with their perception of the value they're getting in real-time.

Why It Matters

Men commit to create, to build, to sustain their foundation. A woman often submits to leverage, gain access, and to ultimately control to that foundation. If she senses your commitment brings her stability, she's in. However, the moment she perceives that her conditional needs aren't being met... Her "submission" has no problem pivoting to someone who can fulfill it, time, loyalty, and or a man's commitment mean absolutely zero to her at That point. This transactional nature isn't a flaw—it's a hardwired strategy woven into her essence. Studies in evolutionary psychology show that women are biologically tuned to seek and secure the best resources for themselves and their offspring, which shapes how they approach relationships, consciously or not. A man's commitment comes from within a decision he's made regardless of the external conditions. He's all in, building his vision, regardless of the odds, that's why understanding this sharp difference will give you power in this modern dating landscape. You'll see the contrast clearly, and you'll know when a woman's investment is rooted in something transactional. Recognizing that lets you approach relationships on your terms not according to social sentiment, or hivemind thinking, knowing that your commitment, once given, is rooted in your drive and your purpose, not fleeting factors that shift with the tides. That's what gives a man leverage— building from a place of unwavering commitment while never losing sight of the conditional nature that often defines a woman's submission.

13 |

MEN ARE GUILTY BY PROXY

Accountability vs. plausible deniability

I n today's world, men walk through the minefield of accountability, often carrying not just the weight of their own decisions but the consequences of others'. Society holds men responsible by default, slapping them with the label of "guilty by proxy." This chapter dives into the gritty reality of how men are held to a standard that demands accountability, while many women operate within a framework of plausible deniability. It's a sharp contrast that shapes the dating landscape, family courts, and even the professional world. Let's break this down. Men are groomed from a young age to "own up," to be responsible for their actions and the outcomes they generate, while women are often shielded by plausible deniability, an "out" built into the social fabric that lets them deflect blame or rationalize behavior when the going gets tough. This isn't about assigning blame; it's about understanding the game men are thrust into and finding a way to maneuver through it strategically. In the tone of Build or Destroy, this chapter speaks directly to men ready to grind through and elevate their lives—by understanding the real dynamics at play.

The Nature of Accountability

Men are wired and conditioned to stand by their decisions. Biologically and socially, they're expected to be providers, protectors, and ultimately, the backbone of stability. Whether in relationships or the workplace, a man's value is often measured by his ability to take on responsibility, and with that comes an inherent level of accountability. You made a choice? Own it. You failed? Take the L, learn, and come back stronger. However, in the landscape of modern relationships, men are increasingly held accountable not just for their actions, but for the outcomes driven by others' decisions. Look at how society reacts when a marriage dissolves or when there's relational conflict. The default is to place the blame on the man's supposed lack of effort, emotional awareness, or some other perceived shortcoming. The man is held responsible not only for his choices but for the shifting needs and desires of his partner—who, in turn, can often deflect the accountability and pin it back on him.

Plausible Deniability: A Shield and a Strategy

Here's the contrast. For many women, plausible deniability isn't just a safety net—it's a strategic tool. This concept, rooted in psychology and reinforced by social dynamics, allows one to deflect accountability by keeping intentions or decisions ambiguous. It's the mechanism that explains why some women may push boundaries, test waters, or engage in complex relational maneuvers without feeling bound to face the full impact of their actions. Take the concept of "playing hard to get" or "keeping options open." From a psychological perspective, plausible deniability provides a sense of control without the obligation of commitment. A woman can navigate situations without openly stating her intentions, allowing her to "explore" without facing repercussions. This same mechanism works in family courts, where women can leverage emotional appeals and societal biases to secure favorable outcomes, often at the man's expense. For men, this means being held accountable not just for what they do but for the decisions made in response to her actions—actions she may later claim as misunderstandings, emotions, or external pressures. We must address Society's Double Standards when it comes to male/female dynamics. Historically, men have been the carriers of accountability in nearly every sphere. From rulers and leaders who faced literal execution for poor decisions, to fathers and providers who took on family responsibilities regardless of circumstance, men have shouldered the blame for generations.

This cultural weight translates into modern life, where a man is judged by what he achieves, produces, and sustains. On the other hand, historically, women operated in a realm where plausible deniability was essential to survival. In societies where a woman's power was often indirect, she had to master the art of influence without direct accountability. This legacy persists today, creating a double standard that is both subtle and profound. Women's decisions are often cushioned by societal sympathy, while men are expected to bear full accountability, regardless of context. I'll go out on a limb and say...rightfully so because as a man, we set the tone, from the beginning. Another striking example of this dynamic is seen in family court, where men face a stacked deck. The burden of proof, accountability, and responsibility typically falls on the man. Divorce and custody statistics show that men are more likely to lose custody, pay higher alimony, and face financial ruin in ways that women don't. Studies on family court biases highlight how men are held accountable for not only their own shortcomings but for the perceived failures in their relationships, regardless of actual fault. In the workplace, men are often expected to perform at a level where mistakes are minimized or masked by tireless work ethic. Women, however, can leverage a social grace or perceived "multi-tasking" advantage, gaining leniency when errors occur, or deadlines aren't met. It's not about ability or intent; it's about the framework society operates within and the expectations it places on each gender.

Embracing Leverage: Moving Strategically in a Stacked System

The lesson here is this: Understand the game and take control. In a world where accountability for men is absolute, and plausible deniability for women is often a given, a man must move strategically. Protect your interests, make informed choices, and recognize the stakes before fully committing. Men must also recognize the value of leverage—establishing legal protections, ensuring financial security, and making choices that minimize vulnerability. When men understand this dynamic, they can reclaim control, operating with a keen awareness of where accountability lies. From prenups and revocable trusts to maintaining independence and developing emotional resilience, men can navigate relationships and responsibilities without falling into the trap of one-sided accountability.

The Science of Accountability and Plausibility

Psychological studies on accountability and decision-making demonstrate that men and women often interpret responsibility differently. A study from Personality and Social Psychology Bulletin highlights how men and women approach accountability: men tend to make decisions based on fixed commitments, while women often operate in an environment of evolving priorities, shifting based on relational context. This doesn't mean one approach is superior; it simply means that for men, accountability is more concrete, and for women, plausibility remains more flexible. A 2023 report in Psychological Science suggests that men who understand and navigate these psychological differences effectively have a better chance of sustaining healthy relationships and avoiding the pitfalls of one-sided accountability. The key is not to internalize societal biases but to recognize them and take strategic actions to protect oneself. In the end, men must remember that they're responsible for their own legacy. Accountability isn't just a burden, it's a strength. When wielded with wisdom and awareness, accountability can empower men to make decisions that elevate their lives and secure their futures. By understanding the contrast between absolute accountability and conditional submission, men can ensure they're building on solid ground, standing firm in a world that often demands more from them than it gives back.

14 | EMBRACING THE TIMES

The versatile man is a Superman

In a world where change is the only constant, the man who adapts, who evolves, and who becomes versatile has the upper hand. This chapter tackles what it means to embrace the times and become the kind of man who doesn't just survive but thrives in any environment. The versatile man isn't a jack-of-all-trades—he's a master of adaptability, a man whose skills, mindset, and strategies can pivot to meet new challenges head-on. The old rules no longer apply. Traditional structures of dating, work, and even family dynamics have been flipped on their heads. The versatile man is the one who recognizes these shifts, learns the landscape, and positions himself as a winner. This isn't about just reacting; it's about proactively embracing the times to become a force of nature—Superman in the flesh. Adaptability equals Power more than just a skill; it's a mindset rooted in resilience. Research from the American Psychological Association highlights that resilience is one of the strongest indicators of future success. The adaptable man uses resilience not only to weather adversity but to see opportunity where others see obstacles. In a 2022 study published in Personality and Individual Differences, researchers found that individuals who exhibit high adaptability and emotional intelligence perform better in fluctuating environments. For men today, this means recognizing that the only sustainable strategy is flexibility. We've all heard about survival of the fittest, but in today's world, it's survival of the most adaptable. The men who thrive are those who can change, shift, and pivot as needed. They're not tied to outdated notions or rigid ideas of success. They're thinkers, strategists, and action-takers, blending traditional values with modern strategies to excel in the rapidly changing landscape. In the past, a steady 9-to-5 job was the backbone of stability. Today, financial stability demands a more dynamic approach. The versatile man builds multiple streams of income, not because he's greedy, but because he's smart. He knows that diversification isn't just for investments; it's for life. A report from the Bureau of Labor Statistics reveals that men who engage in, side businesses or freelance work have better financial outcomes, even in uncertain economic climates. This "grind-and-build" mentality means men aren't relying on a single source to secure their futures—they're creating a portfolio of income streams that insulates them from market shifts. For the versatile man, it's not enough to have one skill; he leverages what he knows to build wealth across various channels. He invests, he saves, he learns new trades, and he's always on the lookout for ways to turn value into income. The man who embraces the times understands that passive income, investments, and diverse skill sets aren't just options; they're requirements in today's market. Strength alone isn't enough anymore. In an increasingly complex world, men need physical versatility—strength, speed, endurance, and adaptability.

Clinical research has shown that physical fitness is directly linked to mental resilience, with a 2023 study from the Journal of Health Psychology affirming that men who maintain regular exercise routines experience heightened emotional regulation and cognitive clarity. The versatile man knows his body is his fortress. He builds strength not just to lift weights, but to endure long workdays, to be resilient under pressure, and to have the energy to keep grinding when others falter. He practices a variety of disciplines, from strength training to cardio and flexibility exercises, becoming a well-rounded, resilient force. This physical versatility isn't just a hobby—it's insurance. When he takes care of his body, he ultimately invests in his long-term ability to adapt and perform, regardless of the demands placed on him. Learn Social

Versatility, i.e., The art of Reading the Room, and Leveraging Connections In a world driven by relationships and social dynamics, the versatile man is a master of human connection. He knows how to read people, recognize intentions, and leverage his social network to maximize opportunities. He doesn't waste time on meaningless connections; he cultivates meaningful, strategic relationships that add value to his life and career. Psychological studies from Social Psychological and Personality Science reveal that social adaptability is a key indicator of success, with men who demonstrate high social intelligence being more likely to excel in leadership roles and personal relationships. The versatile man is a social chameleon. He can move from one social circle to another, effortlessly blending in without losing his sense of identity. This social versatility enables him to gather insights, gain allies, and strengthen his position within any social structure. He's aware that social dynamics are not static; they shift, evolve, and respond to trends. By staying current, he's able to navigate relationships and connections with intention, steering his life in the direction he desires.

Emotional Versatility:
Mental Toughness Meets Emotional Intelligence

Versatility also demands a high level of emotional intelligence. It's not just about toughness, it's about understanding and managing emotions to stay in control. Studies show that emotionally intelligent men have a 20% higher chance of reaching their career and personal goals. Research from Harvard Business Review indicates that men who develop high emotional intelligence are more adaptable in high-stress environments, better able to navigate personal and professional setbacks, and more resilient in the face of adversity. The versatile man doesn't deny his emotions or let them dictate his actions. Instead, he channels them productively. He understands his own triggers and knows how to keep his mind sharp and focused. Emotional versatility means he can remain calm in chaos, stay positive under pressure, and lead with both strength and empathy. In relationships, this emotional versatility makes him an anchor, someone others can trust and rely on—qualities that elevate his value in every social, personal, and professional interaction. Throughout history, the men who achieved greatness were often those who adapted and evolved. Alexander the Great wasn't just a warrior, he was a strategist, an innovator, and a diplomat, adapting his approach based on the challenges he faced. Benjamin Franklin, an iconic figure in American history, was more than a politician; he was an inventor, a philosopher, and a thinker who could pivot between roles effortlessly.

In the modern world, figures like Elon Musk embody this principle. Musk isn't tied to one industry, he's a master of several, from automotive innovation to space exploration to renewable energy. He demonstrates how versatility enables men to create impact across multiple fields. Understand that while I may utilize this figure many times during this book to refer points...he is far from a perfect human, but rather a model for what possible when you fully immerse yourself in your own talents and abilities that make you unique in the world. This adaptability isn't about "doing it all" but rather having the skills, mindset, and determination to adapt to any role necessary. Becoming the Versatile Man is truly the Blueprint for the Future. Versatility is not just a survival skill—it's the foundation of success in an unpredictable world. For men today, becoming versatile means embracing lifelong learning, staying physically and mentally resilient, and navigating social dynamics with intention. The versatile man isn't limited by circumstance; he shapes his own fate by refusing to be confined to a single path. In my previous book, "Build or Destroy: The guide to grinding", I explain how versatility is a form of power, a cheat code to rise above. The versatile man understands that while others cling to the safety of the familiar,

15 |

THE LEGACY WAR

The kids must see you winning

There's no substitute for the power, of "example". If you're serious about your legacy, about the impact you want to leave behind, then understand this: the kids must see you winning, point blank. Not just surviving, not just "getting by"—winning. As a man and most importantly as a father we set the tone for the next generation through action, discipline, and resilience, showing them what true success looks like, feels like, and, most importantly, how it's built...We are the legacy blueprint. Legacy Matters More Than Ever, as We're in a time where the stakes are high. Society is fragmented; the values that are used to anchor us are shifting. Now more than ever, kids need to see solid examples of strength, resilience, and purpose. Legacy is more than a financial inheritance or name on a building. It's the daily display of character, the unwavering commitment to growth, the grit that demonstrates to your children and others watching that anything is possible with the right mindset and effort. Studies in developmental psychology back up the idea that children learn best by observing, after all they are born blank canvases. According to Bandura's Social Learning Theory, kids don't just listen to what you say; they watch what you do. They're internalizing lessons from your actions, your persistence, your setbacks, your comebacks. By modeling a mindset of continuous growth and achievement, you're planting seeds that will shape their perspectives, behaviors, and ultimately their lives, so as parents we must remain mindful of this fact. In one study published in

Psychological Science, researchers found that children who observed parents and mentors setting and pursuing challenging goals developed a greater sense of self-efficacy. They learned that effort and focus paid off, and they internalized a sense of resilience, pushing harder in their pursuits as a result. When your kids see you aiming for—and achieving—big goals, they develop the confidence to set high standards for themselves. You're equipping them with a powerful mindset that says, "If my dad can do it, so can I." This is a dog-eat-eat world we bring our offspring into...that being said, they need to know Winning Isn't Optional, It's Required. This isn't about being flashy or materialistic in their eyes; it's about setting a standard. Winning doesn't just mean financial success, but means mental strength, physical discipline, and emotional resilience. When you win in life, you're modeling for your kids the value of hard work, consistency, and tenacity. You're showing them that life's rewards come from putting in the work, making sacrifices, and refusing to settle, and this fact holds even more true for young boys. When children see you (their first mentor, first teacher, first hero) overcoming challenges, they learn that failure is part of the journey, not the end of it. They see that setbacks aren't permanent, they're just steps toward a bigger goal. This level of transparency teaches them that success isn't an overnight achievement; it's a journey that requires grit.

Leaving More Than Money: A Blueprint for Life

Sure, financial security is important. But legacy isn't about handing them a fat check and calling it a day. Legacy is about giving them a blueprint for success they can apply in any field. It's about passing down mental toughness, discipline, the ability to adapt, and the importance of self-respect. Money can run out, but a strong mindset and solid values are irreplaceable in the grand scheme. Psychological literature also highlights the generational impact of a positive role model. According to a Child Development journal study, children who have consistent exposure to ambitious, goal-driven parents develop stronger problem-solving skills, greater emotional resilience, and a higher likelihood of achieving educational and career success. They're inspired to exceed their own expectations because they've seen first-hand what dedication looks like. Winning requires the right environment, and as a father or mentor, it's your responsibility to create that space. Encourage open conversations about growth, success, and even failures. Share your own challenges so they understand that the road isn't always smooth. By being open about your journey, you show them that the path to success is paved with learning experiences, mistakes, and growth. Let your kids know that certain standards are non-negotiable. Teach them the importance of health, financial literacy, emotional intelligence, and self-respect. Set the bar high and then guide them to reach it, trust and believe they can take whatever tutelage you can dish out. Children who grow up with clear expectations about discipline and excellence are better equipped to navigate life's challenges. By holding them to a standard, you're preparing them for success in a world that doesn't hand out trophies for participation. Powerful family Legacy is often gained Through Resilience, just like powerful family failures are gained through resistance. Psychologist Angela Duckworth's research on grit reinforces this message: success is more about perseverance than talent. Kids need to see resilience in action; they need to witness how you handle setbacks, the way you bounce back from losses, and your determination to keep pushing forward. The truth is life will knock them down. By demonstrating resilience, you're giving them a roadmap on how to get back up, how to fight for what they want, and how to keep moving forward, no matter what. We as steadfast parents should also focus on Passing Down the Intangibles of this life. Your legacy isn't limited to physical assets or wealth. It's in the mindset you instill, the skills you teach, and the strength of character you model. When your kids see you winning, they don't just gain confidence in you, they gain confidence in themselves. They internalize the lessons of resilience, ambition, and the value of hard work.

Case Study: The Rockefeller Legacy

Let's get real about legacy. When we talk about generational wealth, most people picture stacks of cash and assets—but that's only part of it. Take John D. Rockefeller as a case study. Rockefeller didn't just leave his descendants a big fortune; he left them a formula roadmap for discipline, responsibility, and real impact. He knew that money without guidance is just gasoline for a fire that burnt out. His legacy went beyond the bank account. He handed down values, and that's what has kept the Rockefeller name relevant for over a century. If you're serious about building something lasting, take notes. Rockefeller's formula was rooted in a few core principles: discipline, financial wisdom, and responsibility to society. His kids didn't just grow up with silver spoons, they grew up with financial journals and budgets. They were taught how to grow and manage money, not just spend it. They learned early on that legacy is something you must take seriously and protect. Then there's philanthropy. Rockefeller didn't see giving back as just "charity work." For him, it was an obligation. He knew that wealth gives you power, and power gives you the responsibility to impact the world. His family used that wealth to fund institutions and shape policies, and it made a difference. Later generations, Rockefeller-funded hospitals, universities, and research centers are still running strong. That's what happens when you embed your purpose into your legacy becomes unbreakable, like a muscle built through discipline and consistency. There's another side to this story we can't ignore (The Power Play). The Rockefellers didn't just influence education and healthcare. They controlled huge sectors of media and medicine, reshaping industries to align with their goals. The Rockefeller Foundation's influence on healthcare helped create a profit-driven medical industry, something we're still grappling with today. And let's talk about the media. The Rockefellers made sure they had a hand in shaping the narratives Americans consumed, positioning themselves in places that allowed them to protect and promote their interests. This level of influence is a double-edged sword. On one hand, it's genius to leverage what you've built to protect your legacy. On the other hand, it shows how unchecked power can become self-serving, guiding public opinion to fit a private agenda.

Real Lessons from Rockefeller

The Rockefeller legacy shows us what it takes to build something that can withstand time and shifts in society. It's about instilling values that reinforce and protect wealth, teaching every generation to respect what's been built while adding to it. But Rockefeller also gives us a warning: power without checks can turn corrupt. You want to build a legacy? Understand that real impact comes from keeping your principles clean and making sure every generation has the tools, and the vision, to keep it going. If you want a legacy that outlasts you, think beyond just accumulating wealth. Discipline, a sense of purpose, and a willingness to give back are just as critical as your investment strategy. Don't overlook the power of influence but be careful about how you use it. Rockefeller's success—and the controversies around it—teach us that creating real legacy means playing the long game. Real legacy isn't just about what you leave behind; it's about who you raise up and what they're taught to build in turn.

LeBron James sets a modern example of legacy that goes beyond the court. For example, through his I PROMISE School, he's instilling values of education, hard work, and resilience in the next generation. He's leveraging his image and public persona to capture the attention of the youth outside of sports and entertainment. He's showing his own kids—and countless others—that winning isn't just about personal achievement; it's about uplifting others and creating opportunities. James is demonstrating that true success involves giving back and building a legacy that extends beyond yourself. Legacy isn't something you can build overnight. It's a daily commitment, a battle to consistently show up and set an example worth following. Every decision, every action is a brick in the foundation of the legacy you're building for your kids. The world is filled with distractions, temptations, and challenges that can pull you off course. But a man dedicated to leaving a legacy doesn't falter—he fights. Our kids must see us winning. They must see you grinding, being disciplined, overcoming obstacles, and pushing you toward greatness. Because, in the end, it's not just about what you leave behind; it's about who you leave behind. Make sure they're equipped to carry on your legacy, to push the boundaries you set, and to build upon the foundation you've laid. This isn't just about you, it's about the generations that will come after you, inspired by the example you've set. This is how you build a legacy that lasts.

The True Meaning of Legacy Wars – Staying Focused on the War, Not the Battle

In the journey of building a legacy, there will be forces at play that try to undermine, belittle, or even erase your impact, especially when emotions run high, and relationships fall apart. One of the most powerful weapons you can wield is unwavering focus on the war, not the individual battles. As a man, you can't afford to be swayed by attempts at character assassination or by the judgments of the court of public opinion. The legacy you leave isn't defined by one person's narrative; it's defined by your resilience, by your actions, and by the long-term stability and wisdom you instill in your children. For many fathers, the reality of divorce includes enduring legal and emotional battles, and sometimes facing a skewed perception from their own children. Studies show that approximately 50% of children in the U.S. experience parental separation, and nearly two-thirds of them will live primarily with their mother afterward. However, fathers who remain actively involved in their children's lives despite the challenges often witness a powerful shift over time: children, as they grow, begin to see through biased narratives and value consistency, love, and presence. As a father, you must be comfortable with the Long Game, which correlates directly to Persistence and Stability. Men who maintain their course, who continue to show up and put in the effort to be present, are ultimately planting seeds that flourish later. According to research from the Father Involvement Research Alliance, children of fathers who remain involved—even when parenting time is reduced—tend to exhibit greater emotional stability, improved academic performance, and lower rates of behavioral issues compared to children without an involved father. This data is crucial because it shows that, even in limited roles, consistent father involvement pays off in the long game. As a man, your task is to keep showing up, focusing on the values and the lessons you want to impart to your children.

The court of public opinion may lean in any direction, but what matters is your steady presence in their lives, teaching them the power of resilience and being grounded. Maintaining Character Resilience is also key in Shielding Against false and or negative Narratives. Character assassination is an unfortunate reality for many men facing separation or divorce. A study from the American Sociological Association shows that 62% of men feel that their ex-partners attempt to negatively influence their children's perceptions of them. But here's where the difference lies: while a mother may control the immediate narrative, a father can control reality by embodying stability, accountability, and focus. Studies in developmental psychology, like those from the National Responsible Fatherhood Clearinghouse, underscore that child—especially as they grow older—are capable of distinguishing between a temporary emotional narrative and the actual character and behavior patterns they observe. Over time, your children begin to understand the sacrifices, the discipline, and the integrity you demonstrate. They see the battles you fought, the calm you maintained, and the strength you exhibited without seeking validation or retaliation. By focusing on the broader mission, you're teaching them that honor doesn't demand an audience, and integrity speaks louder than slander. The Long Financial Game of Recouping and Surpassing What Was Lost can indeed look and feel like an uphill battle with Mt. Everest in the form of a monetized ex-spouse flexing her court appointed entitlement, just know time is on a focused man's side. Financially, divorce often sets men back temporarily. Data from the Institute for Family Studies highlights that post-divorce, men's economic well-being typically rebounds faster than women's due to their sustained workforce participation and ability to reinvest and rebuild. In fact, while the median wealth drop post-divorce is about 20% for men, research shows that, within a few years, many men not only recoup these losses but surpass their previous financial standing. Men who stay focused, who continue working toward their long-term goals, and who don't let the pain of divorce sidetrack them often find themselves better positioned down the line. By focusing on investments, career growth, and self-improvement rather than reacting to temporary setbacks, these men build assets and a stronger financial legacy over time. Their ability to keep their eyes on the prize serves as a lesson to their children: setbacks are temporary, and success is built on resilience, patience, and planning. The court of public opinion will come and go, but consistency over time is your ultimate advocate. As children mature, they value reliability, empathy, and wisdom more than temporary narratives. Studies, such as those from Child Development, reveal that children with consistent fatherly role models tend to have stronger self-esteem and healthier relationship models. When they see you handling hardships with patience, dignity, and purpose, you're teaching them that true legacy is rooted in character, not perception. So, stay committed to the war. Let them see you winning—not by trying to control the narrative but by staying relentlessly focused on your purpose, your growth, and the example you set. Legacy isn't about how others view you; it's about the values and standards you pass on, and the relentless pursuit of greatness that stands, unshakeable, regardless of public opinion.

The SUM

In today's world, where dating is increasingly transactional and monetized, fathers face a tough reality, especially if they want to set an example of integrity, purpose, and self-worth for their children. The modern dating scene can often be a poor reflection of authentic connection, with a greater focus on material gain, appearances, and superficial compatibility. For a father who's just come out of a divorce, this reality forces a serious choice: Do you spend years trying to find a new partner, battling through a shallow dating culture that might detract from the focus and stability your children need? Or do you leverage the flexibility of monetized dating to stay disciplined, focused, and build a stronger foundation for yourself and your children? Setting the Right Example for your children, especially if you have son's, due to the Dangers and pitfalls of a Monetized Dating Culture. The monetized dating market can undermine a father's message to his children about meaningful relationships, respect, and genuine self-worth. When the dating culture emphasizes instant gratification, transactional intimacy, and a "what can you offer me?" mentality, it reinforces values that often contrast with building a strong family foundation. Studies, like those from the Journal of Family Studies, indicate that children are significantly impacted by how their parents approach relationships after divorce. If they see their father constantly caught up in the superficiality of modern dating, they may internalize that relationships are primarily for temporary pleasure or material gain, instead of seeing a model of commitment, purpose, and real emotional intelligence. Choosing Your Path wisely because the visuals are potent when it comes to Dating vs. Focusing on Self-Growth and Fatherhood. For example, as a man navigating life after divorce, one of the most strategic decisions you can make is about where to invest your energy. Research shows that the median age for divorce is around 30-50 years, and by this stage, many men are amid their careers or building long-term financial stability. Going through the emotional and financial turbulence of dating in a culture that rewards appearances over substance might not only drain your resources but also limit the time and energy you have for the things that truly matter self-care, skill-building, and being the best father you can be. Monetized dating, while far from ideal, does allow one thing—a structured boundary. By recognizing that these interactions are transactional and letting go of the need to chase a partner, you can reclaim time for your self-development. This approach might sound blunt, but it can be the most efficient way to avoid distractions, especially when the aim is clear. It's not about denying the desire for companionship, but about setting boundaries to prevent it from overtaking your purpose or compromising the example you set for your children. When you look at monetized dating as a time-limited engagement rather than a mission, you can free up time to invest in self-care, personal growth, and, most importantly, quality time with your children. Research from the American Psychological Association highlights that single fathers who focus on self-care, career growth, and skill-building post-divorce tend to experience higher life satisfaction and reduced stress levels. Children benefit immensely from this, too. Seeing their father focused on positive pursuits teaches them resilience, prioritization, and self-respect.

You're showing them that it's possible to build a fulfilling, purposeful life that isn't dictated by fleeting relationships or external validation. The other hidden benefit of opting for flexibility in the dating world is that it allows a father to demonstrate the value of patience and long-term planning. By putting relationships on a backburner and focusing on wealth-building, career growth, and skill acquisition, you're not only strengthening your own foundation but also modeling a blueprint of success for your children. Studies on children of resilient, purpose-driven fathers show that they're more likely to adopt strong work ethics, financial responsibility, and emotional resilience. In the end, the choice to minimize dating distractions in favor of personal growth and fatherhood is an investment in your legacy. Instead of burning years trying to find and rebuild love, you can show your children that true worth isn't tied to a romantic partner or external validation—it's built from within, forged by dedication, and lived out by choice. This path not only strengthens you but ensures that the values you pass down to your children are grounded in purpose, clarity, and unshakeable resilience.

16 | THE SABBATICAL OF SUCCESS

Isolate for a Higher Purpose

Sometimes, the biggest step forward is stepping away. Taking a sabbatical—a purposeful period of isolation—doesn't mean you're retreating; it means you're recharging, restructuring, recalibrating. Success requires seasons of solitude. Think about it: real growth, the kind that changes your life, demands focus, and in a world that never stops distracting you, focus is currency. When you strip away the noise, when you isolate yourself for a higher purpose, that's when the real work begins. You start to uncover what drives you, what you truly want, and most importantly, you build the resilience to get there. Isolation isn't loneliness, it's about choosing to stand alone, understanding that every distraction you cut away is another inch gained toward your goal. And let's be real: most people aren't willing to put in that kind of work. They're too busy seeking validation, clinging to comfort, afraid to face themselves and the emptiness that comes with it. Research backs this up. A study from the Journal of Environmental Psychology showed that people who regularly engaged in solitude reported higher levels of self-clarity, reduced stress, and increased creativity. Stepping away from the crowd allows your mind to reset, to escape the constant comparison and superficial demands of everyday life. In solitude, you're forced to confront your own thoughts, strengths, and limitations. And that's uncomfortable, but it's exactly what's necessary to push through to a higher level of success. Purposeful Isolation as a Tool for Mental Clarity because it gives you the mental space to recalibrate, to strip away what's irrelevant and zero in on what matters. This isn't about hiding from the world but rather about turning out the static to hear your own thoughts clearly. Clinical psychology even emphasizes the importance of solitude for mental clarity and emotional well-being. Psychological Review published research that points to periods of isolation as essential for creativity and problem-solving. Without the clutter of constant input, your mind can process more deeply, focusing on complex ideas and solutions that can't be rushed. Look at history. Some of the world's most successful minds—Nikola Tesla, Steve Jobs, Albert Einstein—understood the power of isolation. Tesla would walk miles alone each evening to solve problems mentally, Steve Jobs often retreated to silence to think, and Einstein, famously, spent long stretches in solitude while formulating his theories. They knew that solitude wasn't about withdrawing but about creating a mental fortress where ideas could incubate and mature without interruption. It's a lesson most people ignore, as they're too busy chasing fleeting social heights and empty validation.

The Social Sabbatical: Building Inner Strength

Taking a sabbatical from social dynamics and from constant connectivity doesn't mean you're rejecting relationships; it means you're cultivating the inner strength to return to those relationships with purpose and presence. If you're serious about success, you need to be the type of man who can stand alone. Isolation builds resilience. It's training your mind to thrive without relying on anyone else's support or opinion. Studies show that people who are intentionally isolated to focus on personal goals emerge with a higher sense of self-worth and autonomy. A man who has gone through isolation emerges stronger, centered, and less vulnerable to social pressures because he knows his purpose. It's like lifting weights. Every time you choose solitude over mindless socializing, you're adding another layer of strength. You're choosing long-term growth over short-term comfort. You're investing in your vision, in your future, in a way that no amount of social validation could ever replace.

Isolate for Clarity, Return with Conviction

When you go on a sabbatical for success, you're doing more than taking a break. You're building an edge that most people will never have. You're making a choice to value your goals over the chatter around you. And when you emerge from that period, you come back with clarity, conviction, and a vision so sharp it cuts through the distractions that sidetrack everyone else. People will notice. They'll ask you what changed. The truth is, while everyone else was busy keeping up, you were leveling up. Isolation, when done with purpose, turns you into a man who's unshakeable, a man with depth, and a man with a vision no one can derail. It's about learning to move in silence, to grind without validation, to thrive without applause. That's the kind of power most people will never understand because they're too afraid to be alone. But if you're willing to embrace the silence, to work through the discomfort, you're already a step ahead. Take the sabbatical. Embrace the isolation. Your success depends on it. The noise will still be there when you get back—only this time, you'll be able to cut through it like never before.

17

AGAINST ALL ODDS
Man vs. The Matriarchy Money-Machine

I n a world where the scales are tipped, where the system seems rigged against you, standing tall isn't just an option, it's a necessity. The so-called "Matriarchy Machine" isn't some abstract concept; it's the reality many men face daily. It's the societal structures, the biases, the expectations that can feel like chains. Here's the truth: chains are meant to be broken. First, Understand the Terrain out here, or suffers from landmines and pitfalls. let's get one thing straight: acknowledging the challenges isn't about playing the victim. It's about recognizing the battlefield so you can strategize effectively. Studies have shown that societal expectations often place undue pressure on men to conform to certain roles, leading to stress and mental health issues. But knowing this isn't enough. You must decide whether you'll let these pressures define you or whether you'll rise above them. The Power of Purposeful Isolation is an untapped resource man men refuse to access, usually because of social conditioning, religious dogma, family rhetoric, etc. When the noise of the world becomes deafening, sometimes the best move is to step back. Purposeful isolation isn't about running away; it's about regrouping, recharging, and refocusing. It's about cutting out the distractions, the naysayers, and the doubters. Research indicates that intentional solitude can lead to increased self-awareness and personal growth.

In this space, you can redefine your path, set your goals, and build the mental fortitude needed to face the challenges head-on. You must Build hardcore

Mental Resilience especially if you're going to Face off against the new juiced-up "Matriarchy Machine", understanding it requires more than just physical strength; it demands mental and spiritual resilience. This isn't built overnight. It's forged in the fires of adversity, in those moments when you choose to keep pushing forward despite the odds. Psychological studies highlight the importance of resilience in overcoming societal pressures and achieving personal success. Every setback is a setup for a comeback. Every challenge is an opportunity to prove to yourself that you have what it takes. Re-write your mind and move on Your Terms Society has its definitions of success, but those definitions aren't set in stone. You have the power to carve out your own path, to define success on your terms, and a female should hold sway over none of this at the end of the day. This means setting goals that align with your values, pursuing your passions that ignite your spirit, and refusing to be boxed in by societal expectations. It's about understanding that true success isn't measured by external accolades but by internal fulfillment "first". While purposeful isolation is crucial for self-discovery, remember that no man is an island. Building a network of like-minded individuals can provide support, encouragement, and accountability. Surround yourself with those who challenge you to be better, who understand the struggle, and who are committed to rising above it. Together, you can dismantle the barriers and create a new narrative.

Master and utilize the **"fuck-you principle"** which basically allows you to take negative perceptions and turn them into fuel.

Her: He (A man) needs to make six-figures...

Male translation:

- Focus on your bag (for yourself never for her)

- Focus on learning tax codes, LLC development, entrepreneurship

- Develop useful skills that you can leverage to service others for ROI

- Learn about trust funds (even if you're not ready. Just <u>work towards</u> and stay ready)

- Learn about business credit, and bank ratings

Her: He (A man) needs to be over 6ft tall

Male translation:

- Focus on things you can control: Diet/mental health/hygiene/physical fitness

- Max yourself out (always develop and show up as your best self)

Her: Men should pick better...

Male translation:

- Study the rules of engagement of "Family Law"

- Learn about the family court mafia trust fund system (Title 4D)

- Learn about prenups (if you plan on marriage) and don't waver from protecting yourself.

- Go to counseling or therapy before you start dating

- Reading self-help literature related to psychology/mental health/manipulation/behavior analysis

When a woman throws those standards at you— "He needs to make six figures," "He needs to be over 6ft tall," "Men should just pick better"—don't take the bait and get defensive. Take it as a challenge. This is where the "fuck-you principle" comes into play. Instead of letting these comments tear you down or push you into a proving-your-worth mindset, let them be the fuel that drives you to elevate on every level. Make those "requirements" your checklist, not to impress her, but to maximize yourself.

Let's get one thing straight—building wealth should never be about meeting anyone's standards but your own. If you hear, "He needs to make six figures," don't let it bruise your ego. Flip it and make it about reclaiming your bag on your terms. Focus on generating wealth, mastering tax codes, understanding LLC structures, and building up your financial literacy. Learn entrepreneurship and hone skills that bring real value to others, because that's where true ROI lies. Wealth isn't just numbers in a bank account; it's the freedom and options that come with it. When you're building your financial empire, you're not just hitting her "standards"—you're locking down your independence, securing your own future, and playing the game smart. Look, you can't change your height, but you can control how you show up. Focus on the factors within your power—your diet, physical fitness, mental health, hygiene. Max yourself out. Show up every day as the best version of yourself and see how that changes the way the world treats you. Confidence, fitness, and discipline speak louder than genetics. When you're truly owning yourself, walking in your own power, people feel it. It commands respect and makes you a magnet for opportunities, relationships, and success that align with the standards you set, not someone else's. When you hear the phrase "Men should just pick better," know it's loaded. So, study the rules of engagement for your own protection. Learn family law, Title IV-D, and understand the mechanics of the family court system. It's a business, and it doesn't always have your best interest in mind. So, protect yourself from the jump. If marriage is on the table, prenups and ironclad self-protection aren't just options, they're essentials. Go to counseling, get your mind right, study self-help literature that sharpens your understanding of psychology, behavior analysis, and manipulation. Knowledge is your shield, and preparation is your weapon. Every time society or culture throws out one of these "standards," turn it into a new level for yourself. Each negative stereotype or unrealistic "requirement" becomes another opportunity to refine, protect, and empower yourself. When you're focused on building up your financial independence, maxing out your health and fitness, and protecting your assets, you become untouchable. You become the man who isn't swayed by criticism or validation from anyone, let alone people who don't bring anything to your table.

The SUM

Against all odds, you have the power to rise. The "Matriarchy Machine" may be formidable, but it's not insurmountable. With purposeful isolation, mental resilience, and a clear vision of your path, you can break free from the chains and build a life defined by your terms. It's not about fighting the system; it's about transcending it. And in doing so, you become a beacon for others, proving that no matter what the odds, success is within reach for those willing to grind for it. The bottom line? Use the criticism and demands as fuel, and take them personally, but in the right way. Personal evolution is your ultimate flex, and real power is knowing that everything you're building is for you and your legacy, not for someone else's checklist.

18 |

BREAK GENERATIONAL CURSES
Poison Parental pills vs. Ambitious antidotes

Generational Curses are real fellas, and no one escapes their impact—not even me. I've had to chip away at the mountain of emotional rubble left at my feet by both my mother and father, remnants of traumas and flawed belief systems passed down like heirlooms. Take my father, for example. He spent his life wrestling with childhood trauma rooted in his relationship with his own father. After he turned ten, his father cut him off emotionally and physically. He effectively abandoned him in every sense, and later started a new family on the other side of town. This complete severance of fatherly love and guidance crippled my dad's ability to connect emotionally. Even as he achieved great things, college education, athletic success, and a high-net-worth career—he was silently dragging the weight of abandonment, ultimately letting unresolved pain morph into depression, self-loathing, and self-destructive behavior. Now, I'm not excusing his emotional detachment or his lack of presence in my life, but I took the lessons he left scattered at my feet, learning to navigate life through observing what not to do. Thank goodness I lean toward logic, because if I had been an emotionally driven type, my lifepath would have turned out entirely different. Then there's my mother. She grew up poor on the east side of Detroit, where she was forced to watch my grandmother survive an endless cycle of abuse by multiple husbands. Week after week, the violence she witnessed left scars, and her frustration at my grandmother's choices turned into a deep-rooted resentment for men—long before she even met my father. She adopted an almost militant brand of feminism, shaped by the survival instinct of a woman who saw firsthand the effects of toxic masculinity on her own mother. My mother resented what she saw as weakness in my grandmother, misinterpreting her mother's actions as spoiling her sons, when my grandmother made a hard choice. She could either break her back reining in traumatized young men who, through no fault of their own, had turned to the streets, or she could put her energy into protecting her daughters— knowing they, too, would be vulnerable to men as they grew up. It's essential to understand that these parental scars don't just sit with one generation. Many of our parents, especially those from the baby-boomer generation, were raised by poor, emotionally unavailable parents in a society where dysfunction was normalized. They grew up in unstable homes and communities that knew nothing but survival mode. This dystopian reality created a generation of adults who, in their struggle to succeed or simply cope, often neglected their own kids—millennials like us—leaving us to sift through emotional rubble. Breaking these generational curses isn't easy. It requires facing hard truths, shedding layers of inherited trauma, and building new, resilient foundations. We're the ones left to separate the poison from the antidote, to decide what we pass forward and what we leave behind.

That's where the work starts. We carry the power to end cycles or perpetuate them. Let's talk about generational curses, the heavy baggage some of us carry from birth. Many men are born into families where dysfunction is the norm, a cycle of toxic behavior passed down like some kind of family heirloom. It's easy to get sucked in, to accept that this is just "how things are," but that's the biggest trap. Breaking generational curses means stepping out of that cycle with purpose and making damn sure you're not dragging the same poison into the future. Research shows that children of narcissistic parents often grow up lacking a strong sense of self. Narcissistic parents are preoccupied with their own needs and egos, often disregarding the emotional needs of their kids. Psychologists have documented how narcissistic parents manipulate, criticize, and control to fulfill their own unmet needs, creating a breeding ground for insecurity and self-doubt in their children. As a man trying to break free, you need to recognize the effects of this upbringing on your self-image and address them directly. Therapy, self-reflection, and reprogramming your mind to understand that you are not an extension of their ego is crucial. Generational curses often come dressed up as "realism" or "staying humble." But this mentality stifles ambition and kills any spark for growth. Studies have shown that poverty and low self-efficacy are often passed down because kids learn what they live—they see struggle normalized and come to believe that survival, not success, is the goal. Breaking out of this mentality requires an unwavering belief in your own potential. Look to stories of men who turned nothing into something, who redefined what was possible for their bloodline. Adopt that ambition as your own. Parental envy is real. Some parents view their children's potential as a threat to their own identity, and it shows up in subtle ways—downplaying achievements, creating doubt, or keeping you "in your place." Research shows that this kind of envy creates barriers to healthy self-esteem and self-worth. If you grew up in a household where your success wasn't celebrated, recognize that as their problem, not yours. As a man, you've got to reclaim your sense of pride in what you achieve, because no one else is going to do it for you. Studies repeatedly show that children raised in single-mother households are statistically at a disadvantage in terms of education, financial success, and even mental health. This isn't a knock-on single mother doing their best, but we can't ignore the data. A child benefits from having a father figure, someone to provide structure, discipline, and a sense of accountability. Boys raised without fathers are more likely to engage in riskier behavior, while girls may struggle with self-esteem and boundaries. For men breaking the cycle, the data is a call to arms: Be the father you never had or the father you wish you had. Step up, take responsibility, and give your children a solid foundation to build on.

So, how do you shake off these poison pills and set a new path? Here's where ambition, self-discipline, and resilience come into play. It's about stepping into your role with a warrior mentality, knowing that your battle isn't just for yourself but for future generations.

Face the Truth and Forgive Yourself

Start by facing the truth of your past, no matter how painful. Recognize the ways your upbringing might have limited you, but don't sit in victimhood. Instead, forgive yourself for whatever damage was done. Studies on resilience show that self-forgiveness allows individuals to move forward without the burden of self-blame, a critical step in breaking toxic cycles. You're not responsible for your start, but you are responsible for your outcome.

Reparent Yourself with Discipline and Self-Respect

Part of breaking a curse is reparenting yourself, instilling in yourself the values you never got. Make discipline a core part of your life. Build routines that push you forward—fitness, financial planning, self-education. Research on self-determination theory shows that self-discipline leads to a stronger sense of autonomy and purpose. When you set standards for yourself, you're no longer bound by someone else's expectations or lack of them.

Set a New Standard of Accountability and Honesty

Honesty with yourself and accountability are non-negotiable. When you're raised in dysfunction, deceit often comes as second nature—whether it's hiding your true feelings or playing down your potential. Break that cycle. Be real about where you are, what you want, and what it's going to take to get there. Build a personal code of ethics based on honesty and hold yourself to it. Teach this to your children by example, showing them that integrity is power.

Surround Yourself with High-Quality Connections

Just because you're breaking a family curse doesn't mean you have to do it alone. Look for mentors, friends, and communities that uplift and challenge you. The research on social support shows that men with strong, positive connections have a higher chance of achieving and maintaining success. Cut off relationships that pull you back into old patterns of behavior, even if they're family. Blood might be thicker than water, but progress is thicker than both.

Build a Legacy of Strength and Values, Not Just Wealth

A true generational curse-breaker doesn't just pass down money; he passes down principles. Look at the men who built empires and lasting legacies—not just what they gave but how they lived. Teach your kids self-respect, resilience, and critical thinking. Give them the tools to make their own way and to build on what you started.

Final Thoughts: Breaking Chains and Building Foundations

Breaking a generational curse is no easy feat. It's a grind, a battle against the narrative you were born into. But when you make the choice to rewrite that story, you're setting a new foundation not just for yourself but for every generation after you. This isn't just about breaking free; it's about building something that stands the test of time.

FINAL THOUGHTS
Breadcrumb$

So here we are—at the end of MONETI$ED, a book that isn't just about the game, but about mastering yourself in every corner of it. We've walked through the pitfalls and promises of the modern dating landscape. We've uncovered the myths, the illusions, and the harsh truths about this marketplace. But more than that, we've tackled the core elements of life that fuel a man's growth, his money, his purpose, his legacy. This journey isn't about bitterness. It's not about being jaded, outsmarting anyone, or reducing life to transactions. This journey is about learning to be intentional, to live with your eyes open and your mind sharp. The world around us, especially the dating world, is a place where you'll either step up, or you'll get stepped on. If there's one thing this book should make clear, it's that being a passive player in life is a luxury you can't afford. The "breadcrumbs" I leave here are principles and strategies that won't expire with a trend. They're about setting a foundation you can build on and return to, even as life changes, even as challenges come at you from angles you never expected.

Build Your Legacy

Throughout these chapters, we've emphasized the importance of legacy—not just in financial wealth, but in the character you're building. Legacy isn't something you wait to build when you've "arrived." Legacy is in every choice you make today, in every action that reinforces your self-respect and your vision for a future that outlasts you. You're not here to repeat the mistakes of the generations before. You're here to stand on the foundation they laid, whether it was solid or shaky, and make your mark. Be a man whose presence and principles echo long after you're gone. Let your family, your community, and even the world feel the ripple effects of your purpose-driven life. That's the kind of legacy only the disciplined, the focused, and the intentional can leave behind.

Money, Mindset, and Mastery

Modern dating market, the professional world, and even the landscapes of friendship and family, they all test the same thing: your ability to leverage. To turn your resources—money, time, attention—into tools that elevate your life. There's a reason we talk about "getting to the bag," understanding tax codes, and maximizing every angle of financial strategy. It's because the world doesn't just reward talent, it rewards preparation. The principles we've discussed go beyond just financial literacy; they're about financial mastery. Money is a tool, and every dollar is a decision. Every cent you earn, save, or invest should move you closer to freedom, not just material gain. The aim is to put yourself in a position where your money works harder than you do, where your capital is a weapon, not a burden. With that power, you shape the life you want, the relationships you deserve, and the opportunities that allow you to stand out from the noise.

We've explored self-control, the art of penis discipline, and even the value of fasting—not for their own sake, but as tools to make you stronger. In a world that constantly dangles distractions, man's greatest asset is his ability to master himself. Self-mastery isn't about deprivation; it's about choosing what really matters over what's just easy. It's about keeping your eyes on your goals and recognizing that your time, energy, and mental clarity are far too valuable to waste on fleeting pleasures. Each moment you choose discipline over distraction, you're investing in yourself. You're telling the world—and yourself—that you're not just another man chasing the next thrill. You're here to build. To elevate. To become someone who's rare in a society that's happy to settle. Power isn't about domination; it's about creation. When you've got real power, you can create the life you want without compromise. A purpose-driven man is unstoppable because he knows where he's going, and he won't be deterred by the small stuff. Purpose gives you the clarity to cut through the noise, the confidence to move through challenges, and the conviction to stand firm in your values. Whether you're young or old, whether you've been in the game a long time or just stepping into it, understand that power and purpose are built, not bought. They're built through sweat, sacrifice, and a relentless commitment to your vision. They're strengthened every time you refuse to settle for less, every time you put in work while others are chasing comfort.

Navigating the Future

In today's world, dating, money, and personal growth aren't disconnected—they're all part of the same game. The modern landscape can be confusing, overwhelming, and sometimes downright ruthless. But if you've made it this far, you've already proven that you've got the drive and the resilience to face it head-on. The market will shift. Trends will come and go. What will remain is the man you're choosing to become. Don't wait for the perfect moment. Don't wait for permission. Take these principles, apply them, adapt them, and most importantly, live by them. Life won't hand you a roadmap, but MONETI$ED has given you a compass. Remember, relationships, money, success, they're not the end goal. They're the result of a man who's decided to live with purpose, vision, and relentless determination. Each chapter in this book is a piece of armor, a tool for the battles you'll face. You don't need anyone's validation or approval to step up, just the willingness to grind, to master yourself, and to stay true to the principles that build real power. So, here's my final piece of advice: let every "breadcrumb" you lay down be one that lights the way not just for you, but for those who come after. Set a standard so high that the next generation can look at your life and say, "That's the kind of man I want to become." And remember, you're not here to merely survive or get by. You're here to dominate, to thrive, and to leave a legacy that speaks louder than words ever could.

This is your life -- Live it wisely.